Driven Beyond Success

The True Story That Proves
ANYONE CAN ACHIEVE ANYTHING

by

Edward Primoff

TELEMACHUS PRESS

This book is an autobiography. While the people, places and events are real; some of the names and descriptions have been changed to protect individual privacy.

DRIVEN BEYOND SUCCESS

Cover designed by Telemachus Press, LLC

Cover Art:
Additional cover images used from photos taken by the author.

Interior photos taken by author.

Published by Telemachus Press, LLC
http://www.telemachuspress.com

Visit the author website:
http://www.DrivenBeyondSuccess.com

ISBN: 978-1-939927-98-9 (eBook)
ISBN: 978-1-939927-99-6 (Paperback)
ISBN: 978-1-940745-46-6 (Hardback)

Version 2014.01.08

Printed in the United States of America

10 9 8 7 6 5 4 3 2 1

Dedication

Dedicated to the two most important people in my life; my wife and partner Suzanne, who has made everything I've accomplished possible; and to my daughter Kristina, who has overcome far greater obstacles than anything I've ever encountered.

Table Of Contents

Introduction

The task of writing this book, although done voluntarily, was still one of the most challenging endeavors of my life and probably would never had been possible without the use of speech recognition software from Nuance Communications called Dragon Naturally Speaking. This allowed me to verbally tell my story as it transcribed my words to my computer. Thus, even with my poor reading and writing skills, I was able to tell my life story. Therefore, it is no coincidence that if you feel that the style of this book is as if "I'm talking right to you," I truly am.

The stories you are about to read are true, but a few of the names had to be changed and the reasons for doing so will become obvious.

I am truly thankful to our country for the opportunities it provided me while fully realizing that nowhere else on earth could my dreams have come true. I remain completely optimistic that the spirit of Americans will never diminish and we will overcome any difficulties we face.

Driven Beyond Success

The True Story That Proves
ANYONE CAN ACHIEVE ANYTHING

Prologue

SOMEONE ONCE SAID, "Even more than death mankind dreads boredom." Well at least I have never been the least bit bored. Ed is my name and I am 70 years old. I'm not even supposed to be alive according to a diagnosis at Mayo Clinic in 1969 more than 44 years ago; more about that later. I have lived an incredible life. I think by comparison it would make the fictional Forrest Gump's life seem dull. It has been filled with joy, lots of anxiety, and an abundance of pain, but never boredom, and my life hasn't been fictional.

Like most people, if I only had known early in life what I know now I'm sure my life would have had considerably less anxiety. Contrary to what almost everyone predicted, I've done well, earned lots of money and acquired great wealth, not withstanding unimaginable obstacles. However, there is no do-over button in real life, but hopefully you will find my experiences interesting and maybe even informative and beneficial. I hope so, because that's why I have decided to reduce these experiences to writing and share them with you.

I am living proof that in America anyone can achieve anything they really want, regardless of the handicaps they may have or think they have. I have never read a book with the exception of manuals and textbooks; and only then when it was absolutely necessary. You see, as embarrassing as it is to admit, I graduated high school not knowing how to read or spell even as well as most children in their early elementary school years. When I was a young adult I tried to overcome this by taking reading courses offered by two different reading schools, one I think was named Vicore and the other Evelyn Wood. Testing revealed at that time that my reading skills were limited to about 11 words per minute. Both schools voluntarily refunded my money in the early weeks of the training curriculum. It was only much later that I learned I have an acute case of dyslexia. I see only parts of words so I have to sound out each syllable of each word before I can read or understand what I am reading. It took me over a minute just to read an average sentence.

Throughout my life, it was necessary for me to struggle through required intense reading material to accomplish things I wanted. I now read an average of about 50 to 60 words a minute; still painfully slow. Often I have to read the same sentence over and over and it just takes me an incredibly long time. Imagine traveling through life with that dreadfully awful condition to deal with, especially if you had a strong quest for knowledge as I always have. It made achieving anything much more challenging than it otherwise would have been.

My hope is that overcoming my handicap demonstrates to you that obstacles should never be an excuse for not accomplishing your goals and dreams. You just have to work a little harder. OK, sometimes much harder, but the rewards were always worth it.

Telling my story is the most difficult task I've ever undertaken. I'll try and just start at the beginning.

Chapter 1
The Trouble With Me

EVEN BEFORE MY birth I was trouble. My mother, Betty, had lost both of her parents at age two and spent the next 14 years in an orphanage. At the age of 16 she was forced to leave the orphanage and soon thereafter met and married my father, Charles Primoff, who was also a teenager. Unlike my mother, he came from a family of scholars who were not happy about the marriage.

After graduating college he was drafted into the Army. My mother, having no experience with family life, was left to raise my sister JoAnne and was pregnant with me. She developed a serious kidney problem and was advised that because of complications she probably wouldn't survive if she continued her pregnancy and I should be aborted. My paternal grand-mother, Julie, had her transferred to a hospital with a Catholic doctor be-cause of his position on abortion. My mother did survive and on July 23, 1943, I was born with what was then called an "upside down stomach."

In my early years I was always sick and many doctors told my mother I would not live very long. My father was still serving in World War II. He had been shot through the chest and taken prisoner until the war ended. When he returned in 1945 we moved to a government project for low in-come families called, Shirley Homes, in Arlington, Virginia.

I was very shy and didn't get along well with other children. I was the one the bullies always picked on. The most fun I remember having was going through other people's trash and finding what to me was really neat stuff. One time my sister JoAnne and I even found a whole trash can full of old, partially used cosmetics. We used them like crayons and paint and didn't understand why our parents were so upset with our "artwork."

My father accepted a job with the United States Government as a statistician at the Pentagon in Arlington. He also maintained a part-time job as a hotel manager so I really never got to know him very well. Around 1950, just after the birth of my other sister, Wanda, we moved to Hyattsville, Maryland into a small semi-detached house.

School was very difficult for me. My grades were poor and I don't remember having any friends. Most of my teachers were unenthusiastic about having me in their class and sometimes made an example of me. In the fifth grade my teacher forced me to stand in front of the class and read aloud from a first or second grade book. As the kids snickered and laughed, the teacher said to them that if they didn't take school seriously this is the way they would be. I could be wrong but I don't think the teacher liked me very much.

Later that year she noticed that I had brought a picture book of wild animals to school. She asked to see it and saw that printed on the inside back cover was "Property of Arlington County schools." She asked me where I went to school before moving to Hyattsville. I answered, "Arlington, Virginia." She instructed me to take the book and again stand in front of the class. I tried to explain that my father had purchased the book, but she wouldn't listen. As I stood in front of the class she told all the students that this is what a thief looks like and if anyone is missing anything I probably stole it. That night I told my father. The very next morning he met with the principal and the teacher. He showed them receipts for several books he purchased after the school board in Arlington had discontinued them and offered them for sale, including my picture book. The principal ordered the teacher to apologize to me in front of the class. She did by simply stating she made a mistake about Ed stealing the book. It was much like when some newspapers print their retractions on page "C–21."

In the 1950s I was in junior high school then called the blackboard jungle days, with good cause. It was a very scary time. I was mostly a loner, still had no friends and the bullies continued to see me as one of their favorite targets. I seldom fought back, but on one particular occasion when one of them who thought I was his private punching bag was showing off by picking on me, I said why don't we meet after school and finish this. I didn't really expect him to take my challenge seriously but when I left school that day he was waiting for me, along with several other classmates to cheer him on. A vigorous fight ensued. I was actually a little bigger, heavier, and stronger than him and even though I was not accustomed to fighting, I got him down and held him there until he said he gave up. I thought it was finally over and the bullying would come to an end, but as I got up several of the spectating students jumped me, kicking, beating and knocking me to the ground.

As I struggled to get back into the school I was covered with blood when I noticed that my math teacher, Mr. Stern had witnessed the ambush but made no effort to stop it. Of course arriving home black and blue and covered with blood there was no hiding this from my mother.

That kind of represents the way junior high school was for me. My grades were still poor. When it was decided by the school that I would take general math in the ninth grade my mother and father were furious. At an arranged meeting with the principal my mother insisted that I take algebra because it would be required to get me into college. The principal said to my mother that she was not being reasonable. He insisted I didn't have the ability to understand or pass algebra and that I would never be able to go to any college. Further stating she and my father would have to come to the realization their son basically would have to settle for something much less academically challenging.

Frankly, his assumptions were convincing to me. It was only because of my mother's continued insistence that he ultimately conceded, but stipulated that when I failed he would not transfer me into a general math class and I would be forced to accept the failing grade.

Surprisingly, with the help and encouragement I received from the type of teacher until then I had never been familiar with, I received an "A" in that class for the year. Afterwards, I was assigned all advanced math classes in high school. Yet I still couldn't read well and did poorly in all other subjects.

I don't remember having fun in those years and almost all my free time was spent working after school and on weekends. I did, however, have a love and fascination with airplanes and flying. At the age of 14 I joined the Civil Air Patrol, an auxiliary of the United States Air Force, which had a cadet program that met once a week. I worked extremely hard passing several tests and fulfilling other requirements that included a one-week stay at an air force base. I was told the only food we would receive was at the air force chow hall. This gave me the opportunity to experience military life; more importantly, even though I didn't realize it at the time, it became my first understanding of true capitalism.

I took several dollars from my savings account and purchased candy bars which then cost five cents each. Oh, I didn't eat them; I sold them to the other cadets for ten cents apiece. They had no other way of getting them. I came home with twice as much money to deposit back into my savings. By sheer coincidence I had learned it was far easier to make money by selling things at a profit then it was by doing hard manual labor.

The entire curriculum including the week at the air force base, six courses and passage of final exams took about three years. I received a certificate of proficiency signed by the Chief of Staff of the United States Air Force and received a commission of second lieutenant. Until this time I had never really achieved anything and had always been convinced I never would.

The Civil Air Patrol had become probably the most important thing in my life at that time. I had a few training flights as a student, despite always being terrified immediately after leaving the ground and was certain I could never really fly an airplane by myself.

I was excited about a weekend camping trip that I and other cadets were going on with several senior members. After we returned, I was summoned to have a meeting with the senior commander. I believe he was a colonel. Walter Starling was his name. This was highly unusual as the cadets seldom met with the senior officer members, especially the highest ranking officer.

He stated that he was in the tent close enough to mine to hear what was going on. He accused me of having inappropriate relations with a very attractive young female cadet. I insisted that I had no idea what he was talking about and I tried to assure him I did not did not spend any time with her whatsoever. He obviously heard her with someone else. Nevertheless, he told me he expected me to resign at the next meeting.

The next day I received a call from a senior member who was rather young for a senior officer, about 20. He unintentionally admitted to me, only because he thought I already knew, that he was the one who had the encounter with the young 16-year-old. He pleaded with me not to tell as he said it would possibly mean serious consequences for him, not for me, as I was her same age. I explained the entire situation to my father and his advice was just to do the right thing.

The next week I met with Col. Starling and explained again that it was not me. I never told him who it was. I expected to be discharged; instead I was demoted to sergeant. I stayed in the Civil Air Patrol for about another year and worked my way back to the rank of an officer. Still it was never the same.

Back in high school things weren't going any better. In my junior year, other than mathematics, the only class I did well in and enjoyed was wood shop. I had been working on a project for several months. It was a smoking stand turned on a wood lathe. When completed it was amazingly beautiful. One day when I went to class the smoking stand was gone. A student told me the teacher had entered it into the state competition and it had won first place. When I confronted the teacher he took me aside and told me it was true. Thinking though that it was never going to win, he had entered it in another student's name. His explanation for doing this was because he thought I would never go to college like the other academic student would. His chosen student needed to enter something in the competition to meet his requirements to apply for a scholarship, but didn't have time to do a project. He told me he felt badly that it had won first place and he would in some way make it up to me.

In my senior year, while in an advanced math class, the teacher put a complicated problem on the blackboard and asked if anyone could figure out the easiest way to solve it. There were some very difficult methods, but I immediately recognized that many of the parts canceled themselves out. Therefore, complex methods were not required, you could easily solve this problem in your head. I whispered to the student directly in front of me that it seemed too simple and explained my thoughts to him. He raised his hand and told the teacher my theory while taking the credit for figuring it out himself. I still remember the pride in the teacher's expression as she told him he was the future of our country. I now know these were great lessons as they prepared me for what I would encounter many times throughout my life.

That same year one of my teachers became upset with me. I apparently wasn't paying attention to her and was drawing on a piece of scratch paper. She asked me in front of the class what I was going to do when I got out of high school. I responded, "I'm going to go to college." She and some of the students laughed, replying "You can't even read. How do you expect to go to college or even make a living?"

"I'll tell you what you're going to do; you're going to be a burden on society. Your classmates are going to have to support you one way or the other. You're probably going to be on welfare or in jail, but one way or the other your fellow classmates will have to support you." My response to her practically got me thrown out of school.

At home my father had advanced himself into a prestigious high level position at the Executive Office of the White House. He had become one of the nation's top fuel and energy experts. It was not easy for me knowing I was a great disappointment and embarrassment to him not only in academic and social skills, but also because of the abundance of grief I was constantly causing both of my parents over the years by routinely doing incredibly stupid things. Such as when I took my mother's brand-new mixer apart to see how it worked and never got it back together again. There was a time I was punished and sent to my room which was on the third floor. I tied a rope to my windowsill, climbed out on the ledge and figured I could just slide down the rope and spend the day out. Later I would climb back up and nobody would be the wiser. It just never occurred to me that the rope could break and I would fall about 30 feet to the ground. Not surprisingly, I broke both of my legs, crawled to the front of the house and knocked on the bottom of the door. My mother answered, but not seeing me on the ground shut the door. I knocked again, and when she again opened the door I said "Down here!" That's really all I remember about that episode except that I couldn't walk for about three months; and oh yeah, while I was in bed one night, still unable to walk, I was awakened by my father carrying me out of my bedroom which was in flames. My bed sheet had been pulled into a circular floor fan and had caught fire.

I also managed to embarrass both of my parents at my Bar Mitzvah when I was 13 years old. For those who might not know what a Bar Mitzvah is, it's a Jewish celebration when a boy turns 13 and he supposedly becomes a man. It requires the boy to read certain prayers in Hebrew.

To prepare me for this my father enrolled me in a Hebrew school for about a year. Of course how could I learn Hebrew when I couldn't even read English? Realizing this, the Rabbi gave me a phonograph record to memorize. It would only be one prayer I would pretend to read in the middle of the ceremony.

I listened and practiced almost every day for about three months before the blessed event. I had it down perfectly, but when the big day came it was arranged that a scholarly 13-year-old boy, who was having his Bar Mitzvah too, first came on the stage for about an hour reading many prayers in Hebrew without a flaw. Then it was my turn. I entered and looked down at more than 100 people, about half his family and half mine, and I froze. I got halfway through the prayer and then forgot the rest. After all I wasn't really reading it, I had only memorized sounds. When I stopped I could see and hear my uncle, my father's brother, shaking his head and quietly whispering "uh, uh, uh." Somehow I got through it, but once again I had disappointed my parents.

I'm sure they weren't sorry to see me leave in 1961when I was accepted into summer school at the University of Maryland on a trial basis. I was assigned two classes, English and Sociology. Needless to say it was virtually impossible to pass either of these classes as I still possessed the remarkable "ability" of not being able to read well enough to get through them. After leaving college that fall I didn't know what to do. I was uneducated, couldn't read well, and had no skills whatsoever. I was accustomed to hard work, having had various part-time jobs since I was about 11 years old. I had bagged groceries for a local supermarket, Jumbo Food Stores, and delivered newspapers for what then was called the *Times Herald of Washington, DC*. In the winter, when it snowed, I shoveled sidewalks and driveways and would accept whatever people would pay me. Sometimes I would even get as much as 50 cents. Of course, that's probably like a thousand dollars today. In the summer I cut lawns on a regular basis.

There was never time for fun, but at least I always had money in my pocket and that gave me a unique sense of security. At that time, nothing seemed more important.

After my failed attempt to acquire admissions into the University of Maryland I unsuccessfully interviewed for several minimum wage jobs; I apparently was not qualified for any of them. I was certainly aware of my parent's lack of enthusiasm about having me remain in their home. Therefore, it seemed that there was only one option left; I joined the United States Air Force.

The Air Force recruiter assured me that because of my high math scores I would almost certainly be sent to an accounting school. However, after a few months of basic training at Lackland Air Force Base in Texas, I was shipped to Mather Air Force Base in Sacramento, California.

I was assigned as a driver in the motor pool with a salary of $68.00 a month. On my first day at the motor pool, the other drivers and I were lined up for inspection. During this inspection, a rabbit wandered onto the lot. Noticing this, the inspecting sergeant yelled "Get it!" Several of the airmen chased the terrified helpless animal to the end of the parking lot where it ran into the chain-link fence which surrounded the lot. The rabbit was severely injured and loving animals as I do, it was painful to watch as some of the airmen laughed and continued kicking the injured rabbit. Instantly I realized I was not going to fit in here any better than I did in school and certainly this was not going to be a career for me. I was determined to find the quickest way out, despite having signed up for a four-year hitch.

After extensive research, I learned the only way I could get out of the Air Force early was to acquire 30 college credits while in the service. To do so, there was a program in which I could get out early and still receive an honorable discharge. I signed up for several correspondence courses through several universities as well as courses offered on-base. I also attended Sacramento City College.

Inasmuch as I still couldn't read very well, certainly not well enough to pass any college courses that required extensive reading or spelling, every course had to be in the mathematics arena. Fortunately for me, Mather Air Force Base was an air training command for pilots and navigators. There were several mathematics courses offered right there on the base. I signed up for Calculus, Analytic Geometry, and many other math courses. All of the other students in the class were officers; most were pilots or navigators. Even the one stripe I had, which gave me the designation of airmen third class, had been taken away after I had a very confrontational disagreement with my sergeant that literally resulted in a brutal fistfight. I was now the lowest ranking person on the base.

All the students in my math classes originally thought I too was an officer and had simply forgotten to put the bars on my uniform. Eventually, I became very friendly with many of them and sometimes we even studied together. There were times they would pick me up at the motor pool after my shift and before class. This infuriated my sergeant and he became even more resentful of me; constantly reminding me that I was just a loser taking courses that would never change my status. I was no better than anyone else in the motor pool he would say. On one occasion when I arrived at work, my sergeant called me into his office to say that an airman told him when he arrived at the barracks sometime after midnight he saw me in my room studying. The sergeant stated that the regulations required I get eight hours of sleep every night before arriving at work.

I asked the sergeant, "What did you say to that driver, about getting back to the barracks at that time of the night?" He replied, "That airman was at the airmen's beer lounge, he's allowed to be there, that's why they call it the airman's lounge stupid." I don't recall my exact response, but I remember my frustration. Naturally, he became even more resentful and began changing my shift times making it even more difficult for me to continue taking my courses.

One of my duties as a driver was to pick up officers at the base airport. They were always carrying their uniforms on hangers and often complained about their clothes getting soiled as they would drag on the floor of the box van. On one occasion I picked up a high ranking colonel. As he made the same complaint I asked him why he didn't have a bar welded across the back of the truck allowing passengers to hang up their clothes. He stated that was a great idea and told me I should send that recommendation to the Pentagon in Virginia. He said if changes were made on Mather Base vehicles, it would be a really big deal and I would certainly get an accommodation which was usually accompanied with a cash bonus. He went on to say that if my recommendation resulted in changes to vehicles on all bases, it would be an enormous accomplishment. I would probably get a promotion and a very large cash award as well as possibly even an accommodation presented to me directly by the base commander himself.

A few months after I sent my recommendation to Air Force headquarters, I noticed metal bars exactly as I had illustrated were being welded onto all the passenger van vehicles at the maintenance shop. I immediately approached my sergeant and told him I had sent a recommendation to the Pentagon about installing those bars. He said, "Oh yeah, this came for you a couple of weeks ago and I forgot to give it to you." He opened his drawer and took out a crumpled piece of paper and handed it to me. It simply stated that my recommendation had been accepted and changes were going to be made to all passenger van vehicles at all bases. No promotion, no cash bonus, no accommodation from the commander. Certainly not the parade I had expected. I was incredibly disappointed, but didn't realize it at the time that this experience was one of the best things that could have happened to me. It forced me to work even harder to achieve the requirements I needed to get an early out.

During this first year while attending Sacramento City College I met Geri. She was two years older than me, very attractive, smart and had an incredibly adorable personality. She was studying to become a nurse with the ultimate goal of becoming a doctor. It was not difficult falling in love with her and after we married in 1962, she went to work at a local hospital.

No doubt it was humiliating for her to live in a Sacramento housing project which housed mostly welfare families and a few very low ranking military people like me. Young, handsome interns at the hospital were constantly coming on to her and, needless to say, our marriage ended almost before it began.

I certainly couldn't blame her, as I had nothing going for me. Still, I took the breakup extremely hard. She was not only my first love, but she was also my first real friend and the first person in my entire life, outside of my mother of course, that really seemed to care anything about me.

When I wasn't on duty in the Air Force or taking courses, I worked a second job. I seldom got more than a few hours sleep a night. Most of the jobs were minimum wage. However, there came a time that I answered an ad for what appeared to be a part-time job for a stock clerk at Alcoa Aluminum. The job actually was as salesman for Wear-Ever Aluminum, a division of Alcoa. I told the interviewer I was a very shy person and didn't speak well. I was sure I could never sell anything, but he insisted I was perfect for the job and that I could make lots of money. I didn't know at the time that he received a commission for every salesman he recruited. After getting about $100 out of me for a sample kit, I was hired.

There really wasn't much of a training program. I was told to go out onto a busy street, stop young girls and simply tell them I was taking a survey for Alcoa Aluminum and ask them a few questions. Of course this is something you couldn't possibly do in today's culture, but this was another time and nobody thought anything of it back then. What I would be looking for were single working girls, preferably ones who had started a hope chest, but had not yet purchased their cookware. Then I would tell them that for their participation in this survey they would be receiving a gift from Alcoa Aluminum and it would be delivered to their residence. At that point I was to get their address and set up an appointment to drop off their free gift. When I would show up for the appointment I would give them a free roll of Alcoa Aluminum foil and make a sales demonstration and pitch for a set of Wear-Ever waterless cookware.

The first part, taking the survey, wasn't really difficult, but after making my first appointment I was terrified. I didn't believe it was possible for me to sell anything especially to a young, single girl. I actually had to force myself to drive to the appointment. It became even more frightening when I arrived at the address she provided. This was not an apartment or even a single-family home. In fact, it was a boarding house with young girls coming and going in and out. I thought to myself there is no way I could do this and drove off.

A few blocks away I remembered a Shakespearean quote I had heard on a phonograph record, "Our doubts are traitors that make us lose the good we ought might win by fearing to attempt." I pulled over, took some deep breaths and thought what the heck, I'm not going to sell anything, but what could I possibly lose by giving it a try? I should go back, embarrass myself and get it over with. At least I'll know whether I can possibly do a presentation, after all I had already been conned into buying my cookware samples.

Fearfully, I approached the door and asked for the young lady. To my surprise she actually invited me in and was much nicer than I thought she would be even after realizing I was there to sell her something. Laughingly, her first question was what are you trying to sell me? I nervously told her the division of Alcoa, Wear-Ever Aluminum had just released a new product, stainless steel inner clad over aluminum waterless cookware. Again to my surprise, she was anxious to see it. We went into the kitchen whereby I baked a cake on top of the range and she volunteered to make a pot of coffee. Several other girls became interested and watched the demonstration. Well, I didn't sell one set of cookware, I sold three sets and made considerably more money that very night than my samples cost; even more than a month's salary in the Air Force. I was ecstatic.

Soon I became one of Wear-Ever's top salesmen and I was making an incredible amount of money. I purchased a really cool 1956 mint condition Mercury and soon after that a shiny black 1958 Chevrolet Impala convertible. For a few months life seemed really great, but then someone at the company reported to a local newspaper how much money I was making. The newspaper ran a story that the lowest ranking airman at the base was making more money in his part-time sales job than the base commander by selling cookware. I was called into the orderly room and got reprimanded by the captain in charge. He said that if I was making that much money, the job couldn't be legitimate. I was ordered to quit immediately. I had no choice. This too, made me work even harder at getting the college credits I needed for an early discharge.

I had no education, was separated from my wife and my weight had escalated from about 170 pounds to over 300 pounds. I was never into drugs or alcohol, but I did have the unfortunate disorder of over-eating when I felt anxious or somewhat depressed. Naturally the Air Force had become concerned about the rapid rate I was gaining weight and ordered me to see doctors at the base hospital. My dining hall meal card was taken away and I was given a new one allowing me to eat only at the hospital dining room. Special meals that appeared as if they were meant for rabbits were actually prepared for me. As weeks passed the doctors were confused.

I was not losing weight, rather I was still gaining. What they didn't know was that when I was gaining the weight before being ordered to see the doctors I had anticipated they might take away my dining hall meal card. About a month before being ordered to see the doctors I told the administrator at the orderly room that I had lost my meal card. I was issued a new one, so now I had two. Everyday I would go to the hospital dining room and eat some of the rabbit food. I then would go to the regular dining hall and get the real good stuff loaded with sugar and carbohydrates. I showed them.

Several months later, I had fulfilled all the requirements for an early out and received an honorable discharge. All in all I was in the Air Force for two years, spent entirely in Sacramento. I had no idea what I was going to do. In my mind it was now impossible for me to go back to selling Wear-Ever. I lived alone in a less than 500 square-foot, one bedroom, low income row house in a project called Seavy Circle. I sold both of my cars, the Chevy and the Mercury that I loved so much, and purchased a 1950 Plymouth. This was in 1963, so the car was 13 years old and had long since seen its better days.

I was aware that my parents were not anxious for me to move back home, so I decided to stay in Sacramento and look for a job. Uneducated, unskilled and now weighing over 300 pounds made this a very unpleasant and difficult task. One job I applied for was selling magazines door-to-door. I remember the interviewer as being an older and very attractive woman. She asked if I had ever looked at myself in a mirror. She said because of my appearance, there was no way she could have me out there representing her company, but if something came up in the warehouse where the public wouldn't have to look at me she'd give me a call. Maybe she was just trying to help me.

Eventually I did secure some low income jobs over the next few months. All of them paid less than the minimum wage. Usually they were jobs nobody else wanted and it was difficult for employers to fill them, resulting in low hiring standards. They were all abhorrent to me. I was suffering, so I did what most young people that have gone out on their own and failed do; I asked my parents if I could move back home. Thank God they agreed.

I packed everything I owned into my 1950 Plymouth including my pet Mynah bird that I hadn't mentioned to my parents. The car had recently developed a problem with the transmission and would not easily stay in third gear without physically holding down the shift handle. I proceeded to drive the 3,000 mile trip from Sacramento to Hyattsville, Maryland, expecting to forcibly hold the shift lever in the third gear position the entire way. I actually made it a little over 400 miles before the transmission blew up. I came to a rolling stop at a gas station. I believe somebody upstairs was looking out for me as the owner of the gas station actually had an old transmission that fit my car laying in the back of his shop. After I told him my problem, that I had just gotten out of the military and was trying to make it back home, he installed the transmission for $20 and wished me luck. It held up all the way back to Maryland.

After having the transmission replaced in southern California, the coast to coast trip in the old Plymouth did not go without a hitch. By the time I got to Texas, I already had two flat tires and replaced them with two of the four used tires I had tied on the roof of the car before beginning the trip. I realized I did not have enough money left for gas, let alone food. It was Thanksgiving Day; I was hungry and tired. So, what did I do? Once again I called my parents. My father told me to go to the local Western Union office and wait for the funds he would wire. I was now 20 years old, and still a terrible burden to my parents. I could not have felt worse.

When I pulled up to their home in Hyattsville my mother and father came out to greet me. I couldn't help noticing my father gently shaking his head as he looked at my old car loaded down with all my junk, a Mynah bird in a cage on the front seat, two used spare tires tied to the roof and a son that was about 150 pounds heavier than when he left home two years earlier. They must have been so proud.

Chapter 2
Picking Up Diapers Is A Stinky Job

AFTER MY DIVORCE in 1963, now my most important concern was to get a job in order to move out of my parent's house. The very next day, and for about two weeks, I went on several interviews with no success. All of the jobs I applied for paid minimum wage or slightly above. My father told me the reason he felt I wasn't getting hired was because there was too much competition for those low paying jobs and I should go for a better, higher-paying position. That's ridiculous I said, "What can I possibly do? I have no training in anything." He replied, "You've always been really good at math, why don't you go for an accounting job?" I knew nothing about accounting, but he said accounting is just mathematics; you can do it. I did not agree with my father, but I knew he was very smart and I was not.

Unlike most of the children I know today, even though I didn't agree with him, I did exactly what he told me. I went back to the help wanted section of the *Washington Post* where I found a posting for a junior accountant position with DC Transit. I applied for the job, which required me to take a test before they would schedule an interview. A few days after I took the test the personnel office called and arranged an interview. When I arrived I was told I had gotten a very high score on their test. That made me even more nervous and unsure if I would be able to answer any of their questions. I wondered if I was just going to embarrass myself. What had I gotten myself into?

The very first question they asked was, "What kind of accountant are you?"

I wasn't even aware there were different kinds of accountants. After a short pause I replied, "What kind of accountant are you looking for?"

They said a cost accountant. I responded, "You're in luck." I was hired.

I told my father I had been hired, but I had absolutely no idea how I was going to do the job. He told me again that accounting is just mathematics. He said I would be required to do accounting reports and all I had to do was look at what the person before me had done and just do the same thing except use current figures. Actually, he was right. I did exactly what my father said; posting figures and doing reports was really not difficult at all. However, I was much slower at getting the job done because I first had to learn how the person before me did it by studying his ledgers and reports. I was happy and was making about twice the minimum-wage and even had my own secretary.

After about six months I was called into the vice president's office. In a very pleasant manner he said that after hiring me they realized almost immediately that I was not a cost accountant. He said at first they only kept me on to see what I was going to do. They were very surprised and impressed at how I was teaching myself while on the job. They had no complaints with the accuracy of my work and had originally decided to keep me on. However, they had just purchased another transit company in northern Virginia and they really needed someone who could do the work a little faster. He offered me another position, of course at a lower salary. Crushed, I declined.

I had moved out of my parents' home and into a small apartment, so the very next day it was back to the classified ads. Soon I was hired by a leading laundry service company in Washington, D.C., to pick up and deliver laundry and dry cleaning at private residences. I was assigned one of the 83 routes they serviced. This job paid minimum wage plus a small percentage based on the gross receipts each week. The training program lasted about two weeks. The home pickup and delivery service was from Monday to Friday.

The company though, encouraged anyone wanting to make a few extra dollars to come in on Saturday and a representative would take you to a route that needed to increase its customer base. There you would solicit door-to-door for new customers. For the new customers you secured you would be paid 50 percent of their original bill. This was a good way for the company to build its routes.

Usually only a few employees would show up and I was told generally they would make $15-$20 on a Saturday. I signed up the very first Saturday and acquired many more new customers than they had expected. The new customers' laundry and dry cleaning receipts totaled more than $400. I was excited about making over $200 in just one day. I was really surprised when the company did not seem pleased. The next Saturday again my orders totaled over $400 and the company canceled the program. I was disappointed and confused. Obviously, I didn't think that was a very smart thing for them to do. I didn't make any waves as I was enjoying the job and I also desperately needed to keep it. Realizing my ability to acquire new customers, the higher-ups assigned me the worst of all the routes. In only a few months I had increased its sales so much that I was always in the top three and was making more money than I did as a junior cost accountant.

When I first took over this route, I was working long hours usually getting back to the plant after dark. I came up with a plan to enroll all my customers on a monthly billing process rather than dealing with the cash process which took so much of my time. This allowed me to give much better service and have more time to solicit for new customers increasing my sales substantially. Also, I could work at a much faster pace and get back to the plant earlier and earlier. My route was almost always among the top performing routes in the plant.

I would arrive before anyone else, about 5:00 a.m., but was usually finished for the day by 10:00 a.m. It was a great company and I considered it a great job. I was earning good money for someone only 21 years old and I had almost no pressures whatsoever. I got along with everyone and my bosses were great. I've often said it was the best job I ever had.

After about a year, I was called into the office and told there was a problem. Other route men were complaining about my early arrivals back at the plant. They complained I was making the most money and working the least hours. I told my bosses they should use my successes to encourage and challenge these ridiculous, disgruntled employees to do as I had done. I said they should tell them that if they built their routes to perform as well as I had, they also could get off at 10 o'clock in the morning. They said they couldn't allow that; everyone would be building their routes only so that they could get off at 10 o'clock in the morning. A new rule was announced that no one could come back to the plant before 3:00 p.m., regardless of the circumstances.

Meanwhile, I had been offered a job with a pickup and delivery diaper service company and was told that I could make a lot more money running a route for them. As much as I liked my job at the laundry these new restrictive rules did not make sense to me. I parted ways under very pleasant circumstances and was told if I ever wanted to come back I would certainly be welcome.

The job at the diaper service paid well for those days, but taking it was not a good decision. Picking up dirty diapers and delivering clean ones was nothing like my laundry job. Many mothers didn't know that they were expected to rinse out their dirty diapers, so I would be driving all day in a truck filled with ... you know what. The gentleman whose route I was to take over had given his notice and agreed to train me. On the very first day of training, at about noon, he pulled under a shady tree and turned off the truck. He told me it was lunchtime and he had brought enough for both of us. It was like eating in an outhouse. I had already lost quite a bit of weight while working for the laundry, but I lost considerably more on this job.

At 21 years old, I had lost over 200 pounds, and realized I needed to get a career. I certainly wasn't going to stay with the diaper service. I had been dating an old friend from high school, Jackie Postal. We had gone on several dates and our relationship had become very serious; at least I thought so. One night after taking her home I asked her what she thought I should do with my life. She answered by telling me not to walk her to the door and said that we had to break up. She said she really liked me, but didn't want our relationship to go any further because after getting to know me, she realized the most important thing in my life was to make a lot of money and become financially successful. She reminded me I did not have a college education and no specific skills, therefore my goals were unrealistic and unattainable. All this she surmised while not realizing that I couldn't even read. Money wasn't important to her, but she couldn't see a future with someone who would be chasing a dream he would never attain. She was sure I would just become frustrated and unhappy.

Now I was certain I had to get away from the service occupations and start a career that would give me the opportunity to accomplish what everyone all of my life had told me I could never do—make a lot of money. I had no idea how to do it, so I went to the library and checked out a book, "*So You Want To Be A ...*" Each page outlined a specific career, job description, qualifications, income expectations, etc. I carefully studied every page and learned that almost every career that had a good income potential required at least a college degree. That is, all but one, a salesman. According to the book, salesmen could sometimes actually make more money than occupations that required all sorts of educational degrees. I remembered how well I had done selling cookware, but if I was going to get into selling on a commission basis it only made sense I should be selling something more expensive than pots and pans.

Out came the classified ads once again. I saw a job advertised for a real estate agent. The ad said they were willing to train. It was a good size, well known company and I applied. The owner of the company said he would hire me, but first I would have to get a real estate license which required a tough exam in Baltimore. The company had a training program which I was invited to attend. There were about five people in the class and each student would take turns reading questions aloud. Although I didn't need reading glasses at the time, I always made the excuse that I had forgotten them, never wanting anyone to know I could barely read; especially aloud. I purchased the book he recommended and spent the next several weeks driving around in my diaper truck studying diligently at every available opportunity.

After taking the test in Baltimore, I got onto an elevator with several other people who had also been tested. Immediately people started complaining about the difficulty of the test. One man said he didn't care if he passed or not and said his mother had been in real estate part-time for a year and only sold one house which had never settled. A lady said she didn't know anyone who really made good money selling real estate either. I hadn't heard this much negative talk since the lecture from my captain in the Air Force, but it was nothing compared to what I was going to hear from my father. I had already established that some people were making a really good income by selling real estate. I decided I would pattern myself after those people, not the ones who were failing. Maybe I couldn't be as good as the people who were doing very well in real estate, but I knew I could certainly work longer and harder than anyone else. I decided to find out what the successful people were doing and just try to copy them.

I barely passed the test, with a score of 70. One more wrong question and I would have flunked. I went back to the broker who promised to start me with a draw each week. He asked what the lowest draw I could survive on was and I said $100 a week. He said, "I want you to struggle so I'll give you $70 a week. Let's see how you do," and I was hired.

Excitedly, I called my mother and told her I would like to have dinner at their house that night as I had some very good news to tell them. At dinner I told my parents I had quit the diaper service and was going to become a real estate salesman. To my surprise, Dad became outraged. He scolded me for quitting what he said was a good job. He said it provided me with an income that enabled me to take care of myself. He questioned how in the world I could possibly sell real estate with my limited education and abilities.

"These people are professionals." he said. "How do you possibly expect to compete with them?" He asked me if I could still get my old job back. I told him I didn't want my old job. This was probably the first time in my life I didn't listen to my father. I was scared, but determined.

Chapter 3
Whatever It Takes

TO REDUCE MY expenses, I moved out of my nice apartment into a small rundown two bedroom one; sharing it with a roommate, John Temple, who I met while working for the diaper service. Ironically, our cramped new dwelling was over a laundromat. There were times in the cold winter months when the oil would run out and we would not have heat sometimes for several days, but the rent was very cheap and I needed to keep my expenses as low as I could.

Arriving for my first day on the job, I drove up in an old four-door Chrysler that had been sideswiped on the passenger side. Both of the doors on that side were badly damaged and neither of them would open. I bought it that way because other than the damage it was in great shape and dependable. Due to the damage it was very cheap and was all that I could afford. I was introduced to the other salesmen and assigned my own desk. Of course, almost immediately, other salesmen in the office asked what had happened to my car. I told them, as I would tell my future customers, I had recently been in an accident and was awaiting settlement from the insurance company to get it fixed.

The way most real estate companies operated in those days was that each salesman would be assigned two hours of floor time per day. The company would place ads of listed homes in the newspaper. During your floor time anyone calling on these ads became your customers. If you sold that customer a house you would receive one-quarter of the total commission and the listing salesman would receive one-quarter. The company would receive the other half. I asked the broker "How do you get listings?" He told me that you usually just talk to acquaintances and ask them if they knew anyone who wanted to sell their house. My problem was, other than my parents, I didn't know anyone that owned a house. I was only 22 years old.

On my first day, after waiting by the phone for two hours, with absolutely no calls, I left the office and drove directly to a nearby neighborhood. I spent the rest of the day knocking on doors, one after the other, asking whoever answered if they knew anyone who wanted to sell their house. After about seven hours of getting one no after the other, somebody surprised me by actually saying, "Yes, we want to sell our house." She invited me in and I got my first listing. When I brought it into the office the next day, my surprised broker asked me if I knew these people. I said, "I do now." I didn't want him to know that I had canvassed the neighborhood as in those days it wasn't very classy or expected that real estate agents would solicit door to door. I suppose they thought that was reserved for vacuum cleaner and Fuller Brush salesmen.

Over the next 30 days, I found myself working 14 to 16 hours a day, seven days a week. I had averaged a listing or a sale almost every day, more than all the other salesmen combined. Before even completing my first month, the broker called me into his office and told me I needed a better car. He offered and I accepted his practically new gorgeous Thunderbird. I had not established a credit rating, but his guarantee allowed me to take over the balance of his payments which now was not a problem as he had raised my draw from $70 to $125 a week.

Things were moving very fast and I really didn't know what I was doing. I was young and stupid. Propelling me forward was simply hard work, enthusiasm, a burning desire to succeed, and most of all, an absolute fear of failing and having no place else to turn. The training was poor and I began losing a good many of my deals. Still, I was making a good income and more than covering my draw.

About six months after I started at this company, I ran into an old high school friend, Frank Childrens. He too had gotten into real estate. We compared notes and I found that even though I was doing well, he was making considerably more money and working a lot less. I was working for a big company with a well known name and I had a beautiful desk in a modern first class office. He, on the other hand, was working for a company I had never heard of and it was in the dumpy basement of a residential house that had been converted to a small office building. He had an old metal military type desk that was in terrible condition. Frank and the broker, Ted Gehring, were the only employees of this company. I had heard of a really good salesman named Jack Darling with another company had recently passed his broker's test and was going to become an associate broker at Gehring's company just until he could get his own established. I had also heard that Darling was really great at closing a deal and almost never lost one after writing it. I wanted to find out how my friend was making so much money; more importantly, I wanted to learn from Darling. Gehring was anxious to hire me and offered me a draw of $175 a week.

The draw increase was especially helpful as I had recently gotten remarried and was expecting a child. I had lots of new expenses. Although it seemed risky, the career move was a very good one for me. I was counting on receiving a few thousand dollars from my former broker for commissions that were earned over and above the draws I had received. Even though I never got paid any of it, changing companies and working with Darling was a good decision. Unlike me, he was very soft-spoken and mild-mannered and before asking for anyone's signature, he had a way of making them feel comfortable and confident. He was far more professional than the other real estate salesmen I had been working with and it was easy to see why people liked and trusted him. In learning how to emulate him, I soon was not losing my listings or sales either. He was truly a great mentor.

As for my friend Frank, I learned what he was doing. He was a terrible salesman and seldom listed or sold any homes on a commission basis. Instead he would outright buy the houses and sell them himself. The profits far exceeded what the commission would be and many people were happy to get an immediate sale and settlement. Although this is common today, it certainly wasn't back in the 1960s. In fact it was harshly denounced by our local board of realtors.

Frank also had a distinct economic advantage over me. He had been left a substantial inheritance and could afford to buy the houses himself. I, on the other hand, had little savings and lots of new expenses. Nevertheless, learning the procedure of how to do it and make a profit enabled me to purchase a lot of houses for the company. They were making huge profits and I would be paid only the commission, but I was content.

Due to the new revenue that Darling and I were generating, the company decided to expand. They rented space in a modern commercial office building. The primary broker, Gehring, asked me to train new recruits and help him build the company. Over the next year I trained several salesmen usually by taking them with me and letting them share in my commissions. I didn't mind, for I was always the company's top producer and still was more than covering my draw. Within about a year the company had added about six or seven salesmen all of which I had trained and all of them did pretty well with one exception, Dave Horn. He was nonproductive and would come into the office on Sundays and watch football on television all afternoon, distracting me and the other salesmen. I had no choice but to put up with it as he was a good friend of the broker who had hired him.

One morning I came in and I could see by the faces of the salesmen I had trained that there was something wrong. There was a letter on each salesman's desk stating that Horn had been made sales manager and we would be taking all of our scheduling and assignments from him. I picked up the letter and marched into the broker's office. Before I could speak, Gehring said, "Let me explain. The company has grown and needs an office manager. Naturally, one would expect you to be given that position and I considered it. However, you are the company's top producer. I feel it would be unwise to take your attention away from the main objective of creating sales." He also reminded me that Horn was a college graduate and this was a good image for the company. Whereupon I reminded him I had trained every salesman in the company at my own expense, giving up thousands of dollars in commissions. I told him if anyone was entitled to be given the position of sales manager and receive an override on the salesman's commissions, it should be me. He replied that the decision had been made and I would just have to get used to it. He knew I had recently spent most of my savings on a new home. I was now married with a daughter and had lots of expenses. He was certain I would do exactly what he said "get used to it."

At first I didn't respond. We stared at each other for a couple of minutes and no further words were spoken. I turned around and walked out of his office. It only took me a couple of minutes to clean out my desk.

Before I left Darling stopped me to wish me luck and said, "Ed you're going to have a brilliant career in real estate." This was the first time anyone had ever offered any words of encouragement in my entire life. He recently died and I will always be regretful of not having the opportunity to tell him what a positive influence he made on my life.

I drove directly home and told my wife what I had done. She was very upset and asked what I was going to do. I answered, "I have no idea." The next morning, after getting virtually almost no sleep, I received three telephone calls. They were from brokers who had heard about my departure and each eagerly offered me a position. The best offer I received was from a broker named Jim Biggs. He had purchased and operated some of the largest real estate companies in the county and everyone in the industry had great respect and admiration for him. He offered me a position as sales manager, doubling my draw and increasing my commission rate, as well as an override on every salesman.

I accepted his offer and did well there, but after about a year I knew that it was time for me to take the giant step of opening on my own. I passed the brokers test in 1968 and opened my own company, Prime Homes Realty, working out of my house.

The pressure on me was now greater than ever. For the next several months, I worked longer hours every day, almost always seven days a week. The last thing I needed was a major setback, but then again somehow I found the time to do something really stupid.

I had learned from a teenager in my neighborhood how to make extremely loud firecrackers. He showed me where to order the chemicals and how to mix them. My closest friend, who by the way was a detective, and I would throw them off of his high-rise balcony. How dumb was that?

One day after mixing a batch of chemicals in a four cup Pyrex pitcher instead of using a wooden spoon to fill the cartridges as I had before, I forgot and used a metal dinner knife. This instantly caused a terrible explosion burning off all of the hair on my head, face and arms. The pain was almost unbearable. I ran out of my house and instantly lost my eyesight.

I was ambulanced to the hospital and rushed into a room to be examined by an eye specialist. He asked me what happened. I remember thinking, what's worse than being blind? Being blind and being in jail. Making firecrackers was illegal. I told him I had recently bought a house and found a jar of black powder in the basement. I said that when I opened it and stuck a butter knife in to smell, it blew up in my face.

He asked if I knew what was in the powder and I told him I did not. "That's too bad," he said, "if I knew what was in the powder I could possibly save your eyesight." Without hesitation I told him what chemicals were in the jar and the exact proportions.

I heard him laugh and say, "So you were making firecrackers."

I asked, "Am I blind?"

"No, not permanently. Don't worry; I'm not going to turn you in. You're going to suffer enough through the treatment that will be required."

Every day for about a month, I went through a painful procedure performed by an eye specialist. Thankfully I regained my eyesight. I went right back to work after first throwing out all of the firecracker supplies.

Now I was working harder than ever. My family life suffered terribly, but financially I was doing well, although once again, I was gaining substantial weight. I had no idea of how much the pressure would soon be increased when something that nobody could have possibly predicted happened. The federal government raised the interest rate on mortgages higher than the legal rate of the state. I had several pending settlements which now could not settle. Salesmen throughout the county were leaving the industry and taking jobs elsewhere and several real estate companies closed. After losing all of my pending deals and exhausting my savings I realized I also had to secure a salaried job somewhere, at least until the state could rectify the problem. I now had the responsibilities of a family.

During that time, I took a job working for United Laboratories as a sales representative. The job lasted only a couple of months. It paid extremely well, but required extensive traveling which made it impossible to consummate even the few deals I still could do that didn't require new financing. After only a couple of months I left U.L. and took a job with the local Sears Roebuck store selling air conditioners and refrigerators. The pay was much less, but the job only lasted about three months.

My weight had escalated to almost 400 pounds. My blood pressure had also become very high and I had developed a serious abnormal heartbeat. I was seeing a well known heart specialist, Dr. Michael Halberstam in Washington, D.C. On one occasion, as I was waiting in his office for my appointment, I picked up a magazine. On the cover was what I remember to be a picture of the very thin and attractive daughter of William Bendix, an actor on a TV show called the "Life of Riley." Inside was the article about how she had lost several hundred pounds by having an experimental operation. I took the magazine into the doctor's examining room and showed him the article. He explained to me that this was a new experimental intestinal bypass procedure that, to his knowledge, had not yet been performed in the United States. He said it was very dangerous, untested and he was very much against it. However, after a few weeks of my constant insistence, he gave in and found a surgeon who agreed to perform the operation.

After having the procedure, I immediately began to lose massive amounts of weight, although I was developing serious lightheadedness resulting in several epileptic type seizures over the next few months. My mother convinced me to schedule an appointment with Mayo Clinic. After extensive testing they told me they too were very much against the operation I had and that it was irreversible. They further stated that I would develop many medical problems with my liver, kidneys and other vital organs over the next few years. They told me, in no uncertain terms, it would be very unlikely for me to live past the age of 40 and nothing now could be done about it. At that time the intestinal bypass operation was in its infant stages and totally unlike anything done today. Mayo Clinic did however correct the seizure and lightheaded problems by giving me massive doses of magnesium, potassium and other minerals that had been greatly diminished as a result of the bypass operation.

By now the state had finally solved the interest rate problem by raising its rate so that it matched the federal rate. I had lost over 200 pounds and was anxious to get back into real estate full-time as soon as possible. After all, I now believed I didn't have many years left. I wanted to open a professional real estate company with an office and hire and train my own salesmen. I had managed to save a few thousand dollars, which was way short of my ambition. I applied for a loan to several banks, but all of them turned me down including the Small Business Administration. I did, however, manage to acquire the money I needed from what is called a private hard money lender. Their interest rate was considerably higher than the bank's rate and was secured with the equity in my home.

If the current Dodd-Frank legislation had been in effect at that time this would not have been possible. The government would have had to protect me from myself; not allowing me to risk my home as collateral. I might still be selling refrigerators at Sears today.

While preparing to open my office my father called to share an article in the *Washington Post*. There was a program being offered by the Naval Propellant Plant just outside of Washington, D.C. There were positions they needed to fill and if accepted into this program they would pay a small salary and all of your college engineering training. After completing the training you would be obligated to work for them for a certain length of time. I told my father that my dream was to open my own real estate office, while he insisted this was a once-in-a-lifetime opportunity and it would give me security for the rest of my life. He convinced me to just take the test; by stating that I possibly wouldn't pass it anyway. I took it along with a few hundred others that wanted this "once-in-a-lifetime opportunity."

The test was solely mathematics and frankly I did not find it the least bit difficult. Afterwards, I was called in for an interview. I was told that I had gotten one of the highest scores and was going to be accepted into the program. I struggled for a couple of days with the dilemma of what course my life should take. This was probably the toughest decision I ever had to make. I never told my father I had been accepted into the program.

While in the process of planning to open my office, I received an unexpected call from Bob Scarpulla. He was my manager at Wear-Ever Aluminum when I was in Sacramento. We hadn't spoken for about seven years and I was thrilled to hear from him. He asked what I was doing and told me he was looking for something to get into following his ensuing retirement from the Air Force. I told him about the opportunities in real estate and was surprised he agreed to uproot his family in California and move across the country to become my sales manager. He had no experience in real estate sales or even a real estate license, but he was the best salesman I had ever worked with and I knew he would make a great sales manager. He made the move, passed a real estate salesman's test, and helped me open my office. A brand new phase of my life was about to begin.

Chapter 4
Mister Faster

THE BUSINESS BECAME rather successful after we opened the office in Lanham, Maryland in 1970. I hired and trained several salesmen and most of them did well. Bob was always among the top ten income earners in the Prince Georges County Board of Realtors. I continued to work as much or even more than ever, spending more time with my business than I did at home. This may have been good for the success of the company, but it was certainly not a recipe for a successful family life. Soon, JoLynn, my wife, and I separated, and subsequently divorced.

I had managed to borrow enough to open my company, but not nearly enough to finance the homes that we were purchasing and remodeling. I had become friendly with a very wealthy real estate tycoon, Sol Peters. He agreed to finance all of our real estate purchases and as a result of our friendship, wouldn't even charge me interest. Instead, he would only take one-half of the profits from the sales he financed.

What a good friend he was to offer such a kind gesture. His returns actually amounted to several hundred percent of his investments. Peters was very pleased and I really had absolutely no animosity about the amount of money he was making as there was nowhere else I could have acquired the necessary funds. I would have not been able to purchase the particular homes that he was financing. The number of our brokerage deals far exceeded the number of homes we purchased and resold. (For those not familiar with the term brokerage it means, "Selling other people's homes on a commission basis.") Even though we sold far more homes on a commission basis than the homes we purchased, the commissions were very small compared with the profits we made on the homes we purchased, remodeled and resold.

Peters was a member of an exclusive club called the Progress Club. The club was made up of primarily older, successful businessmen who met regularly to socialize and play cards. I would often go to the club with him, even though I didn't gamble or play cards, because to do so was beneficial to me and to my company. I was young and energetic and several of the members asked me to handle their real estate affairs, but going to the club wasn't just about getting business. Most of the members were at least 40 years my senior and I got a remarkable education just by listening to them.

On one occasion, I overheard a conversation in which two members were talking about what it was like in Germany in the late 1930s. I interrupted them and asked, "Did I hear you say that you were there and some Jews actually supported Hitler?" He responded, "Yes, some did." I asked, "Did you?" He said that he was very young at the time, but he remembered his father arguing with another Jewish businessman about the dangers Hitler might bring to Germany. He told me the same Jewish businessman responded by saying, "Hitler's good for business, how bad can it get?" Those words I have never forgotten and they changed my political ideology as I came to realize how precious and fragile our freedom is and must never be taken for granted.

Beyond work, there were only a few things I did for enjoyment. One of them was to take flying lessons. I was so very scared every time I went up. At first I was certain I could not complete the lessons and obtain a pilot's license, but I was determined to try. It had been a dream of mine since adolescence. I thought it might be a good idea to purchase a small airplane, thinking this would force me to complete the lessons. After about 20 hours of instruction, my instructor told me that I was ready to go solo. I disagreed, but he insisted. After taking off on my very first solo flight that morning I remember how afraid I was and thinking if I could just land safely I'd never go up again. This was just too frightening and I was prepared to give up. Following a perfect landing, I realized it wasn't so difficult or scary after all. I went up again and made another perfect landing.

On my third takeoff, I was rather confident and my fear of flying had disappeared. On my downwind leg in the pattern, the airport controller called me on the radio and told me to land immediately and to come in to see him. I thought, "What did I do wrong or is something wrong with the airplane?" What was the crisis that would cause him to call me on the radio on my initial solo flights? I became a little nervous again but landed okay. After I quickly tied down my airplane I rushed to speak to the controller. He told me that my office had called and said it was very important for me to call them as soon as possible. I did and one of my salesmen, Harry Trowbridge, said he wanted to know if he could go home early. That's about how things went with some of my office staff. Despite similar interruptions I managed to get my private pilot's license and went on to earn a commercial license with multi-engine and instrument ratings and ultimately became a certified flight instructor.

The only other hobby I enjoyed was photography. I had been taking and developing pictures since I was a very young boy. Only on one occasion did my father take me to the White House and my most prized possession became the picture I took of President Lyndon B. Johnson, which now sits in a frame in my office. I had purchased one of the very first 35mm cameras on the market. To this day I even have a picture of every house I ever sold.

On one occasion Bob Scarpulla and I were on our way to a listing appointment in southeast Washington driving down Pennsylvania Avenue. We heard gunfire and then we saw a man running from the bank with a cloth bag in his hand. It was like something out of a gangster movie. The police arrived from several directions almost immediately. I grabbed my camera, jumped out of the car and laid on the ground. I took continuous pictures and captured a frame of the policeman shooting the bank robber in the back as he tried to run away with the loot.

When the entire episode was over, I called the NBC News Department. I asked if they were interested in the photos I had taken. They said they were and asked me how much I wanted for them. I replied that I would have to get the film developed and they could send me whatever they thought was fair. Just bring us the undeveloped film they said. I immediately drove there and dropped off the undeveloped roll of film. One of my pictures was shown along with the story that night on local television and possibly nationwide. They sent me a check for $10.

That is when I realized photography had to be for enjoyment, not income. I would stick to real estate.

As for my real estate company, although I was earning a great income, I was spending most of my time every day handling numerous problems. Purchasers with "buyer's remorse;" sellers thinking they were never getting paid enough for their property; sellers not wanting to comply with repairs required by the buyer's lender; appraisals coming in short of the agreed sales price; and so on, and so on. The problems were endless and settlements seldom went smoothly.

I was always operating at a breakneck pace and my friends nicknamed me "Mr. Faster." No matter what I was doing, I was always in a hurry to get it done. One of my salesmen, Gary Web, told me he had separated from his wife just after purchasing a very expensive boat. He said he had put several thousand dollars down and wondered if I would be interested in buying it and taking over the payments. He suggested it would be a great way for me to relax, something he said he had never seen me do. I said sure and told him I would like to take the boat out this weekend and we would do the paperwork on Monday.

I hooked up the boat to my new Dodge pickup truck. What could possibly go wrong? Brand new truck; brand new boat. Making a gentle right turn while traveling on Route 424, I noticed what appeared to be someone trying to pass me on the left. As I looked to see what kind of idiot would be passing me on a turn I saw it wasn't an idiot at all, it was my brand new boat.

Living up to my reputation as Mr. Faster, I didn't take time to secure the safety chains. After all, I was only going to go a very short distance. When I had slowed down to make the turn, the trailer with the boat on it had become unhooked from the truck and was now passing me. It went off the road to the left and down a steep hill. I pulled over and watched. It looked like the boat would come to rest in a large vacant field, but the trailer and boat made every turn just right so that it crashed into an old partially buried locust post. The boat was fiberglass and it shattered as if it were a light bulb. All that was left was a dented up trailer, a motor sitting on the ground, and thousands of small particles of fiberglass.

I ran to a nearby house and called Gary. I asked him if he had insurance on the boat.

He asked, "What happened to the boat?"

"Gary, there is no boat. Do you have insurance?"

After calming him down and telling him what had happened he told me that he did have insurance. He had not signed the title over to me and thus the boat was still his. We turned a claim into the insurance company. They paid off the boat and I was saved, I thought, until the insurance company sued me for wrecking the boat.

In December 1972 my father was admitted into the hospital for a scheduled minor operation; at least that is what the doctors told us. Only hours after being advised that there was nothing to worry about he died from unexpected complications at the age of 54. Naturally, I took his death very hard.

By the end of 1973 I had managed to save a substantial amount of money. I met with my accountant and learned something very interesting. We were a pretty good-sized company now doing hundreds of settlements a year on a commission basis. I had purchased, remodeled and sold only a little over a dozen houses that same year. After paying the salesmen their commissions and all of the expenses I had made only about 10 percent of my income from the brokerage and about 90 percent from the sales of the houses I had purchased and sold. Yet, more than 90 percent of my time and almost all of the problems were spent on the brokerage part of the business. The decision I ultimately made was not a difficult one.

For about three years I had been dating a wonderful girl, Sue. She had been very supportive and I knew she would support any decision I made. Bob had made an incredible amount of money, more than any other salesmen I knew. I realized he was anxious and ready to open up his own company. With the shocking death of my father, I fully realize how quickly life could come to an end. I was tired; it seemed as if I had been on a treadmill all of my life and I was always aware my time was counting down. I began to develop the symptoms that the Mayo Clinic had predicted. Without telling anyone I sent a memo to each salesperson stating that there would be a sales meeting for January 2, 1974, and they would be required to attend.

Everyone thought this meeting was a kickoff to begin the new year. They were shocked when I announced that I was closing the office.

Bob did open his office and my salesmen all transferred elsewhere. I moved into a brand new large stone home in Scaggsville, Maryland, and established my new office there. I thought I might make somewhat less income, but I really didn't care. It now became more important for me to spend more time with Sue and my daughter Krissy who was now 7 years old. The first year at this new location I spent my productive time purchasing homes, having them remodeled and selling them. For the first time ever I had lots of free time and surprisingly my yearly income more than doubled. Things were working out just great.

Chapter 5
Angel On My Shoulder

IT WAS 1974 and for the next couple of years things went pretty well. I was purchasing lots of homes and now had my own crew to completely remodel them. I had accumulated a very healthy savings. I didn't need to borrow funds which resulted in considerably higher profits. I purchased a high performance Beechcraft Bonanza single engine airplane. Sue and I spent much of our time flying and I was really enjoying a great life.

There were some minor inconveniences. I was testing a twin engine Cessna 310 airplane. One of its engines had just been overhauled and the maintenance shop at the airport gave me a list of procedures to perform at different altitudes and different engine power settings so the final inspection could be signed off. Phyllis Wilson, a friend and also a pilot, asked if she could go along and sit in the co-pilot seat. Sue sat in the back. The plane flew flawlessly. After completing all the procedures successfully we headed back to the small Suburban Airport in Laurel, Maryland. Phyllis asked if we could land at Baltimore-Washington International Airport as she had only experienced landing at small fields. I called approach control and received a clearance from the tower to land on Runway 28.

While on final approach, at about 2,000 feet, a control cable broke and the airplane attempted to flip over. Stabilizing the plane and keeping its wings level was only possible by lowering the nose and increasing its speed which far exceeded the airplane's maximum landing speed. Reducing power would cause one wing to rise radically making the plane uncontrollable.

Maneuvering the airplane was only possible by using its engines. I did manage to touch down right on the runway numbers, but our speed exceeded 200 miles an hour.

When I pulled back on the power, the airplane yawed sharply to the left, went off the runway and headed directly toward the airport's high voltage antenna system. The brakes were engaged at maximum pressure. The field was very dry and dust billowed on both sides of the airplane which to us looked as of it was smoke. Sue pulled the emergency window release. We were still doing somewhat over 100 miles an hour and it appeared to all of us that there was no avoiding the large antenna system now only a couple hundred feet directly in front of us.

Before we took off, the airplane had been fueled with over 100 gallons of gasoline in two large tanks, one at the end of each wing. We all had the same thoughts of impending doom. Just before crashing directly through the fence surrounding the antennas the right landing gear dropped into a large gopher hole, broke off, and stopped the airplane instantly. Technically the airplane was totaled but we were fine. Sue and I were flying our Bonanza by the end of the week, but I don't believe Phyllis ever flew again.

Sue saw an ad in the newspaper for a Crown Pawnbroker auction of unredeemed jewelry that was being held in Washington, D.C., at Kamin's Auction Gallery. I told her that it was a waste of time. I explained that pawnbrokers surely know the value of what they're selling and you're not going to get any bargains. Her desire to go was stronger than my desire not to and I agreed to go to this auction only to prove to her I was right.

At the auction we did make a few purchases. I purchased a man's ring with a large red stone for $100. I had no idea what it was, but I was bored and the ring was in a heavy 18-karat gold setting. Engraved inside were the words, "Tiffany & Co." and it had a serial number, so how could I go wrong?

Over the next few weeks some of my friends would tease me about what they called the "jellybean ring." I decided to find out about the red stone ring. I learned there was a well-known gemologist, Tony Bonanno, in Silver Spring, Maryland. He examined the ring and asked what I paid for it. I said, a hundred. He said that was a good buy and asked if I wanted to sell it. I said, no it was only $100 and I kind of like the ring.

He excitedly said, "Did you say one hundred dollars?"

"Yes."

"Do you know what you have?"

"I only know what you tell me. I know nothing about jewelry."

He told me that my ring had about a 40 carat Burmese, pigeon blood red, star ruby of exceptional quality. He said the value was well over $100,000. Now, I really didn't want to sell my "jellybean ring." Sue and I both instantly realized that some pawnbrokers didn't have knowledge of gemstones or even of their value. This could be a great opportunity for us. We both enrolled at the Columbia School of Gemology and graduated as certified gemologists.

We also learned about the simple metal value of gold and silver. At that time silver was only selling for about $4.00 an ounce. We started going to the auctions every week. I was amazed at the amount of sterling silver that we bought at much less than its intrinsic value, especially when it was in bad or dented condition. I didn't know how or where to sell it, but I knew at the prices we were paying it was a good investment. I just kept buying and storing it.

By 1976 I was doing well enough to keep about a third of the houses I purchased. This gave me additional income from their rentals. Sue and I spent every day together, sharing time in all our endeavors. She even took flying lessons and got her private pilot's license. I could not have had a better partner or friend. That year we married.

Krissy had already become very close with Sue. For several years we had my daughter almost every weekend and all summer. It seemed as if we were set for life. If only my health could hold out and so far it had. It seemed just too good to last and naturally it didn't.

My ex-wife also remarried and moved to Virginia about an hour away. Unfortunately, things did not go well there. My daughter developed serious problems with her new family. It became impossible to continue working as all of our time and attention was directed solely to resolving the situation. Our income pretty much ceased and our expenses for doctors, lawyers and court costs were overwhelming. Financially we survived because I had substantial savings, but we had to sell most of our rental properties. The situation ended after about 18 months when custody was changed and my daughter moved in with us. We immediately began working long hours to recover from our economic losses. It only took about a year to recover financially.

This terrible situation was finally over, but we were about to encounter another serious setback. My health began deteriorating at a rapid pace as my entire abdomen had deteriorated. My stomach became extremely enlarged, my skin turned a bright orange color and my lips were yellow. I ended up unconscious at the Howard County Hospital looking as if I was wearing clown makeup. The doctors recommended immediate surgery to try to repair the damage. After scheduling the surgery, my wife insisted I get a second opinion at Johns Hopkins Hospital, in Baltimore. There I was fortunate enough to see Dr. Thomas Hendrix the chief gastroenterologist. He advised me to immediately cancel the surgery, stating there were very few doctors who understood the complications of the experimental operation I had received years before. He said there was no repair for my condition and I surely would not survive an operation to try to repair it. Dr. Hendrix said my current problems were caused by the high-carbohydrate, low-fat diet, that my current doctors had prescribed. Explaining that my digestive system was now different and I did not absorb fats. In fact, my cholesterol levels were critically low and corrected my current situation by simply reversing my diet; high-fat and low-carbohydrates.

Naturally, he became my permanent doctor and a really good friend. I regained my health and went back to work.

Real estate was our primary source of income, but dealing with precious metals and jewelry was a lot more fun and did generate some income. Sue and I would often go to antique shows and flea markets sometimes acquiring really incredible deals on jewelry that had values far exceeding the dealer's asking price. More importantly, we were accumulating large quantities of sterling silver. On one occasion we went to an antique show in Upper Marlboro, Maryland. We were walking around filling paper grocery bags with sterling silver. When we bought hollowware pieces they were always damaged or in very bad shape. We smashed them to make them as small as we could in order to fit more of our purchases in the bags. We each had two bags almost completely filled when we ran into a friend, Stan Hall and his wife. He was a successful builder. He owned a multi-engine airplane very similar to mine and sometimes we flew together. He asked, "What in the world are you buying?" as he looked in the bags. I responded by saying, "We're just collecting some old silver."

That night we had dinner plans to meet another friend, Alan Stein, at my house. He too was a pilot and a good friend of Stan's. When he arrived I was in the process of weighing the silver I had purchased that day. Curiously, Alan wanted to see how it worked. I showed him what the total weight was and the value at the current price of silver. The total intrinsic value of that day's purchases was about $8,000 and my total receipts were less than $3,000. He said he was shocked.

About two weeks later Alan called and said he had a funny story to tell me. He said last night he had dinner with Stan who told him what a shame it was about me. "I thought Ed might have problems, but I had no idea how bad it had gotten for him," Alan said Stan had told him. "What are you talking about? Ed's doing great." he said. Stan replied, "No Alan, I ran into him at an antique show, he and his wife were running around buying up old dented pots and pans." When upon Alan asked him if that was about two weeks ago. Stan said it was and Alan told him he was at my house that night and it was sterling silver I had purchased, not pots and pans. He told him I had spent about $3,000 that day and the value of the silver was about $8,000. Stan replied, "There's no way Alan; that stuff was all dented up."

This kind of explains why it was easy in those days to do what we were doing. Very few people understood the intrinsic value of silver, surprisingly even many dealers. Of course, you couldn't profit that much every time you went to an antique show or a flea market, but you could always make something and it was really fun.

In 1979 we were doing pretty well once again, but the country was doing poorly. Jimmy Carter, who I supported and voted for, was President. Only on certain days could you purchase gasoline. Even when you could there were long lines and the prices had soared. Inflation was into the double digits and the prime rate of interest was skyrocketing and soon would exceed 21 percent. Mortgage companies were closing and friends of mine working for these companies were losing their jobs. One friend closed his mortgage company, drove home, pulled into his garage, closed the door and left the car engine running, killing himself. Times had become terrible and we were all very worried.

In December of that year, I received a telephone call from Al Denman, an acquaintance, who had a wholesale jewelry business in Washington, D.C. We had done some business together over the last couple of years and he knew I had been collecting silver. He said someone had brought him a large bag of rivets and claimed they were 90 percent silver and left it with him to be checked. He said they wanted $16,000 and he didn't know what to do with all the rivets. Sue called Capital Metals, a refinery in Baltimore. They told her to bring them in and they would assay them for us. After assaying a few of the rivets they determined they were in fact, 90 percent silver. I asked where I could sell them. After weighing the rivets they wrote me a check for a little over $24,000. Al and I split the profit, $4,000 each. I thought, "What a great business."

Times were hard and real estate sales were almost nonexistent. Jewelry stores, including Al's, were just struggling to survive. I told Al that we could go into business together. He had all the jewelry store connections and I could finance the operation. Al thought it was a great idea and again another new venture began.

Chapter 6
All That Glitters

IT WAS 1980 and my new enterprise began just after New Year's Day. The price of gold and silver was also rising rapidly. Only six months ago, the average price of gold was $275 per ounce and this month it would reach $850 per ounce. Silver which had been trading for about $4.00 per ounce would soon reach over $50 per ounce. Al contacted several jewelers and was able to purchase a good amount of scrap gold. He brought it to me and I would give him the cash he had spent as he needed it for the following day's purchases. Of course it was up to me to sell it. Al told me he would have a load every night.

Each day's quantity amounted to several thousand dollars, but was never large enough to sell directly to a refinery. Sue quickly found a small company in Gaithersburg, Maryland, that was purchasing gold at what the owner claimed was 94 percent of its market value. Calculating the value of scrap gold jewelry is actually very simple. It's elementary arithmetic. It is almost always marked with the karat. For example, 14-karat is 58.5 percent pure gold; 18-karat is 75 percent pure gold and so on. When he cut me a check, I told him the amount was somewhat less than I had figured. He said he'd been in business for over 35 years and he knew what he was doing. "Everyone sells their gold and silver scrap to me," he said.

The following day, the same thing happened. My check was short. He argued that often gold is not always what it is marked and he could tell just by looking at it. So the next day, I purchased a gold testing kit and separated and tested every piece before delivering it to him, but again my check was short. I told him I had tested every piece, I was correct, and he was not really paying 94 percent as he quoted. He reminded me again that he had been in business for over 35 years and everyone within several hundred miles was selling their gold and silver to him.

Sarcastically he said, "Who else are you going to sell to?"

"You're forcing me to open up and compete with you."

He responded arrogantly, "Good luck."

The following morning Sue contacted Capital Metals in Baltimore, the small refinery that had originally assayed and purchased the silver rivets. They agreed to refine and purchase our gold and silver as long as we had at least 25 ounces of gold at a time. They agreed to pay us 96 percent of its total value. Every night Al's quantities became larger and larger. We were making an incredible amount of money. At the end of the first month I told Al I would need a copy of his accounting records. He said he had none. I told him I could not operate that way. I had a pretty good size real estate portfolio once again and great relationships with several major banks. My records needed to be immaculately maintained. I told Al he had made a considerable amount of money and surely had put enough away for at least one day's purchases. He could still make his purchases every day and I would pay him 94 percent in cash every night. Al really liked that idea as he would make considerably more and I would make considerably less but I couldn't risk the possible consequences of continuing to operate as we were.

I owned a house on the corner of a major intersection in Prince George's County, Maryland. It had recently been re-zoned from residential to commercial office space and was vacant. What could be more perfect? We immediately opened in this building and installed a sign that read, "Highest prices paid for gold and silver—DEALERS WELCOME." The response was overwhelming. The price of precious metals was still rising. Gold and silver dealers were popping up everywhere. Small dealers usually were buying only four or five ounces a day and they needed to sell it on a daily basis to replace their cash for the next day's purchases. The word spread quickly that we were actually paying an honest 94 percent and almost every local dealer began selling to us.

It was more than Sue and I could handle by ourselves. We hired a young man named Sergio to be our manager. He was a goldsmith we knew well and his talent and good character was exemplary. We also hired several employees that we quickly trained. Three of them were real estate brokers I had worked for a few years earlier, but now with the economy as it was they were glad to have an income. Within just a couple of months we were purchasing precious metals every day from hundreds of dealers. Al was also expanding his business in Washington, D.C., and was selling us larger quantities than anyone else.

There were concerns throughout the industry that many wholesale gold buyers were issuing bad checks which frightened many of our dealers. I understood these concerns as we ourselves had received over $100,000 in returned checks from Capital Metals. To overcome this we began paying everyone with cash. This resulted in us acquiring even more dealers; some from other states. I had to make special arrangements with local banks to have available the large quantities of the cash we needed; sometimes, as much as $100,000 a day.

The large volumes we now were doing enabled us to deal directly with Johnson Mathey Refinery, one of the world's largest and most respected refineries. They agreed to refine and purchase our precious metals and pay us 99 percent. Because they were in Toronto, Canada, I purchased a practically new twin engine turbocharged Cessna 310 airplane and made all the deliveries myself. Ultimately, our volumes became so large that it was possible to sell directly to Engelhard refineries in New Jersey. By flying the deliveries to Newark it made it possible for me to be back into the office in less than three hours. Sue and Sergio ran the office every day until I returned. We would close at six o'clock and drive directly home. Dealers that couldn't make it to our office during the day were always waiting there with their metals to be weighed. We seldom got to bed before midnight and never got more than four or five hours of sleep a night. We were working seven days a week.

Precious metal prices had risen so rapidly we felt confident that this could only last a very short time. After all, how much scrap gold and silver could there be before the supply was gone and the business would end? I had made good money in real estate over the past several years, but nothing like this. We were not like one of our dealers who said, "This is the greatest business I've ever been in. Everyday I work I make over $500, so I only have to work one day a week."

Robberies of jewelry stores and pawnshops increased substantially. There were frightening reports of wholesale gold buyers not only being robbed, but tortured and killed as well. A dealer reported missing in Florida was found mutilated and buried in a shallow grave in Georgia. The business had become increasingly dangerous. We instituted a policy that required all employees to arrive and enter our office at the same time while I sat in the car with a shotgun for their protection. Sergio would then stand in the doorway, also with a shotgun until I was securely in the building. We also installed sophisticated alarm systems and two-way, bulletproof mirrors between offices. I contacted our local county police in Hyattsville and invited them to visit with us often. Sue had the great idea of bringing in doughnuts every morning and putting a roast and a turkey in the oven every day. It provided lunch for us so we didn't have to leave the building and there was almost always county police cars present in our parking lot. Our security was about as good as it could possibly be and we never had life-threatening experiences at this location.

One of my main concerns was that some of our dealers may unwittingly be purchasing stolen gold and silver items. The last thing I needed in my life was to be charged with purchasing stolen goods. Sue and I had become good friends with the police detective in charge of our area and explained to him this serious problem. We helped sponsor a local bill, which later became state law, that required all dealers to identify, describe and report all precious metal purchases to their local police department and hold the items 30 days.

Our support for this bill angered many of our dealers. Some argued they would have to give up items that they paid for and would lose their money. I explained to them that if anything they purchased had been stolen, there could be a risk that they would be charged criminally. I also reminded them that we were all making a lot of money and if any of the items they purchased were stolen they should be happy to give it back to its rightful owner. Most of them agreed.

Actually, almost all of our purchases were from dealers. We were not required to itemize or report these transactions as the dealers had already done so at their location at the time of their purchase. We did, however, make some purchases every day from the public and those we reported as required. The entire time we were in that business I don't believe the police recovered even one item from the daily reports we gave them. Often, when I suspected an item may be stolen and if it had any identifiable markings such as a gold school ring, I would contact the owner myself and give the item to the police so it could be returned. Many times arrests would follow. Both Sue and I took great pride and satisfaction in returning stolen items back to their rightful owners and we gained respect from the local county police. Many of them ultimately became really good and lifelong friends. We benefited greatly from this relationship and their special effort each and every day to look out for us.

We continued working seven days a week sometimes earning as much as six figures in a single month. After four or five months it seemed as if the supply was endless. I purchased a small commercial building in another part of the county and opened a retail operation that purchased only from the public. Things did not go well there. We purchased large amounts of precious metals from this new location and were making good profits, however we could not maintain the same level of security. After the second armed robbery, we closed that location and sold the building. Although we didn't have that trouble at our main office, there were many other problems.

All of our time was consumed with the precious metals business which left no time to manage our real estate rental portfolio. We interviewed several people for a full-time position to manage our real estate rentals. The job was pretty simple and didn't require experience. Mary Lee, a young lady I interviewed, expressed how badly she needed this job. She said she recently had a child and her husband had left her. I told her that I really wanted to help her because of her desperate financial condition. I was concerned about her working in our office where there was so much cash and precious metal activity. She insisted she could be trusted and asked me to just give her a chance. I felt so sorry for her and discussed the possibility of her employment with Sue and Sergio. Against the objections of both of them, I hired her. Everyone in the office soon came to like her and she seemed to be doing a good job. We gave her many raises and in just a few months she was earning considerably more than her original salary.

On a Friday night just a couple weeks before Christmas a tenant called me at my home and said he had dropped his rent off at my office and forgot to get a receipt. He had been a really good tenant for a very long time. He always paid his rent with cash and was a stickler about getting a receipt. He asked me if he could come by the office the next morning and pick it up. Normally, I would just ask Mary to send him a receipt, but it was Saturday and she didn't work weekends. The next morning when I went into the office, I immediately checked the ledger and it was properly posted. She had done a good and proper job as I had expected but I noticed something amiss. There were bank deposits made but his was not included. I called Mary at home and she told me she had included his cash with the other check deposits but had forgotten to write it on the deposit ticket and the teller failed to catch it as well. She went on to say that she realized it as soon as she got home and she had just called the bank and was told not to worry; the teller would catch the mistake on Monday when he balanced his station. She said, "I will go by the bank Monday morning and pick up the deposit receipt, unless of course the teller is a thief and keeps the money."

"That's great I'll see you Monday." I realized instantly she was lying. First, that particular bank was closed on Saturday and therefore she couldn't have talked to anyone there. Secondly, tellers don't total their books the following business day; it's always done immediately after closing their station.

I had dinner that night with our police detective friend and told him what happened. He had a good laugh and said, "I told you so. You're never going to be able to prove she took the money; just get rid of her." I bet him a dinner I would get a confession out of her. Monday morning I had a friend call and ask to speak to me. Mary told him I would be in at any moment. He told her a little fib for me; that the bank teller had denied there was any cash deposited and they were at that moment giving him a polygraph. He said if the teller passed the polygraph, they would be coming to my office so all of our employees could also be tested. He asked her to give me that message.

When I arrived at the office it was obvious she was very nervous and raced into my office to tell me of his message. I calmly responded, "I expected that." She asked, "Why are we getting a polygraph?" I told her not to worry; it was only because there was a bank involved and I had insurance that would cover the small loss. The bank teller would probably fail the test anyway and it would end there. Tears began to run down her face. She told me she had never stolen anything before. She said she felt so bad because we had been so good to her, but she had no money for Christmas and it was such a small amount of money to us.

I truly believed this was probably the first time she had stolen anything and it really was a very small amount of money. I wanted to give her a second chance. After having her sign a full confession I took four $100 bills out of my pocket and handed them to her. I told her to go out to her car and come back in and tell Sergio she was embarrassed because she just found the money between the seats of her car and had simply forgotten to deposit it.

"You're not going to have me arrested or even fire me?"

"No, everyone deserves a second chance. No one will ever see this confession unless you steal something from this office again."

She asked me not to tell anyone and she would never do anything like this again. The next week she told Sergio I was the kindest person she ever knew.

I did of course tell Sue and Sergio and I asked them to keep it confidential but watch her very carefully. Both of them strongly expressed their dissatisfaction with my decision. My detective friend was a little stronger, calling me an idiot. The week after Christmas, Sergio confronted me with news that he noticed that some of the scrap gold was missing. He said he went through Mary's trash can and found it wrapped in newspaper. I checked the rental records and she had not deposited another cash rental payment. I couldn't believe it. When I called and confronted her she hung up on me. I spent the rest of the day going through the rental records for the past year and found there was about $12,000 missing.

I called my detective friend who, after laughing, sent two policemen to her apartment to arrest her. They said her apartment was beautiful and she had all new furniture. After her sentence, as they led her out of the courtroom, she passed us and looked directly at Sue, and said, "I'll get you for this." She spent two weeks in jail. The judge had ordered her to pay restitution. We never saw or heard from her again. Nor did we ever pursue restitution.

In November 1980, Ronald Reagan won the presidential election. Neither Sue or I were ever politically active, but we always voted. The economy was still doing very poorly and although it seemed as if we were working in a pressure cooker all year, we were still making a lot of money and things were going extremely well for us. Even so, our concern about the terrible economic conditions throughout America far outweighed our desire to continue making so much money. With this new president, there now was renewed optimism throughout the country that the economy would soon recover. Sue and I shared this optimism and were looking forward to the coming year. We hadn't a clue of how another twist in our lives was about to happen.

Chapter 7
You Have The Right To Remain Silent

AS 1981 BEGAN our precious metals business slowed considerably. It was, however, relatively steady and we were still making a healthy income. I only delivered the metals to the refinery about once a week. This provided me with the opportunity to take advantage of the greatly reduced prices in the real estate market as they continued to fall dramatically and were down as much as 30 percent. Our net worth was increasing rapidly and I was investing most of the profits from the precious metals business in new rental properties. Sue and Sergio now handled most of the daily business activities themselves.

Shortly after the inauguration in January, I received a call from someone in the White House stating a very good friend of President Reagan had his solid gold money clip stolen from him during the inauguration. They said it was a gift from the President and described it as having the Great Seal of California on the front and an inscription on the back which read, "For friendship above and beyond. Love, Nancy and Ron." They told me they had knowledge I was purchasing gold from many area dealers and I had a reputation throughout the law enforcement community of locating stolen items so they could be returned to their rightful owners. They asked if there was any possibility I could recover this item as President Reagan himself would be very appreciative. Sue and I spent several hours that day calling dealers and finally located the money clip at a dealer in Montgomery County, Maryland, just outside of Washington.

I called the White House the very next morning and told them I had recovered the money clip for them. I was overwhelmed with excitement when I was personally invited to meet with President Reagan at the White House. CBS News learned of this and filmed me pulling up to the East Gate at the White House and ran the story that night on their news broadcast. To this day, hanging in my foyer, is the picture of Ronald Reagan with his handwritten inscription thanking me for the special effort we took to recover the money clip for him and expressing his appreciation.

Although my net worth was now into the good seven-figure range and I still maintained a very healthy income, I hadn't shaken my long established insecurities. I always had an underlying feeling that at any time all this could come to an end. My lifestyle hadn't really changed very much. I didn't eat at expensive fancy restaurants and seldom did I see the inside of an expensive clothing or department store, unless of course there was a big sale. Sue was still cutting out coupons and they knew us well at McDonald's and K-Mart. Sue and I shared a philosophy of saving and investing. We avoided any unnecessary or wasteful spending.

I knew that filing my tax returns unnecessarily late could result in penalties which would really be a colossal waste of money. I called my accountant several times requesting he prepare my tax returns as soon as possible. I explained we had made an incredible amount of money and I needed to know what my tax burden was going to be. After repeated requests from me and equally repeated delays by him, he finally arrived at my office the first week in April. He reviewed our records and was shocked by the quantity of transactions we had made and the profits our company had generated. He worked every day for the next two weeks but could not complete our returns by the April 15th deadline. They were filed one day late.

When I called him about a letter I received from the Internal Revenue Service stating I had a penalty fee of $14,000 for being late he quipped, "That's nothing to you, your income was seven figures, just pay it."

At that time the tax rates were considerably higher. After we paid the federal, state and local taxes we retained somewhat less than 30 percent of the total revenue we generated. Even so, our retained earnings that year were more income than I had ever made before or even anticipated making.

That same year I received, in the mail, a questionnaire asking a lot of personal questions including a request for the amount of my income for the prior year. It came from a committee that was organizing our 20th high school class reunion. It stated the people that answered the questions would be kept anonymous and the information would only be used to announce successes and calculate the class's average number of children, income, etc. Inasmuch as the questionnaire was to be returned with the payment for the reunion, obviously whoever received it would know who answered the questionnaire. My income for the prior year reached into the seven figures and I thought it rather pompous and unwise to reveal that information. I was going to leave that question blank until Sue convinced me to answer the question with a simple "$100K plus." I didn't remember most of my high school classmates, but there were a couple of students I really did like and one young lady I had dated. I thought it would be nice to see them.

When Sue and I arrived we were seated at a table with several couples, none of whom I knew in high school. One of them suggested we go around the table and introduce ourselves and tell what we were doing for a living. I remember one as saying he worked for the County Department of Education. Another said he was a supervisor at the post office. They seemed like really nice people, but I had not known them in high school and now had very little in common with any of them. It appeared none of the few people I wanted to see were at the reunion and I desperately wanted to leave. I really wasn't feeling very well anyway and was not anxious to engage in conversation with the strangers at our table. When it came my turn to introduce myself, I simply said my name and surprised even Sue by saying my occupation was an IRS auditor. I assumed this would pretty much assure the other people at the table would not want to engage in a conversation with me and my assumption proved correct.

The evening became considerably more unpleasant, as I was eating my dinner, I felt a draft under the table. I pulled my chair out a little and looked down. I had gained a considerable amount of weight recently, but I didn't buy any new clothes. Like most people who gain weight, I felt I would soon take off the excess pounds. The zipper on my tight pants had pulled itself apart and there was no fixing it. My new permanently opened area was about the size of a grapefruit and naturally exposed my underwear. As inconspicuously as I could, I alerted Sue of my awkward predicament. She put her hand over her mouth trying not to expose her uncontrollable laughter. I couldn't wait to get out of there.

Before we could leave, the announcements were made which included the results of the questionnaire. Now I was really worried about how I had answered the questions. What if they announced my name as being the top income earner and I was asked to stand. What would I do? First they made several announcements about the average number of children, how many people were still living in the area, and those sorts of trivial matters. They finalized the announcements by saying the average yearly income for the class was somewhat over $17,000. They concluded with; even though the questionnaire was to be anonymous they thought it appropriate for the person who had done so well to proudly stand. Sue handed me her evening program and signaled for me to hold it in front of the opening. Fortunately, we both were very relieved when it wasn't my name announced. It was actually someone I knew, a local businessman who had earned about $60,000 that year. After the announcements I said, "Let's get out of here as quickly as we can."

As we were leaving one of the ladies who had worked on the reunion committee approached us, "We saw your answers to the questionnaire but knew you were just kidding." I gently smiled and without saying a word continued for the door.

I couldn't believe the evening could get much worse and we almost made it out before I heard a female voice say, "Ed you better not leave without saying hello to me." I instantly recognized the voice. It was the one person I really wanted to see that night and the primary reason I had gone to the reunion in the first place. I had dated her for a short time in high school and considered her a really good friend. I hadn't seen her for over 20 years, but I had a serious dilemma. My zipper was still pulled apart and I was holding Sue's program in front of the opening. Sue and I walked slowly toward her table all the time holding the program in the appropriate place to conceal the opening. She introduced her husband and I introduced Sue. I was standing while she was sitting which made the program I was holding at her eye level. I told her I'd love to stay and chat but we were late for an important engagement. She asked me to call her so we could make arrangements for the four of us to get together and I told her I would. She took a pen out of her purse and said that she didn't have any paper as she reached for my program. She wanted to write her telephone number on the program, but I had a death grip on it. Pulling back, I told her I had her number. Her husband looking puzzled saying, "Our number is unlisted, how do you have it?" I replied that I had unlisted numbers and I would tell them about it when we got together, but I was so late I had to run.

Sue did not stop laughing the entire drive home. At least one of us enjoyed themselves that evening.

Al, our former partner, was still delivering very large quantities of gold and silver scrap. He was exceptionally bright, but I became concerned about his behavior. He was slowly becoming erratic, arrogant and rather nasty. He was completely unlike the person I had known for the last several years. Sue and I suspected he might have started using drugs. I was even more concerned about the quantities of precious metals he continued to bring to my office, while other dealers were gearing down, Al was increasing his staff and bringing us even larger quantities. I found myself often lecturing Al about the importance of making sure that everything he bought from the public was reported as the Washington law required and explaining what the consequences of not doing so could mean. Al usually had a flip response with something like, "I only buy stolen stuff at night, because the policing agencies are so stupid and they always go home at five o'clock, so I'll never get caught." I would get mad and tell Al that's not funny. He would respond saying, "I'm only kidding. What happened to your sense of humor? You know I would never buy anything knowing it had been stolen." He always insisted he was reporting all transactions, but his business kept growing and his quantities were getting larger and larger.

Al even hired a new office manager, Ken Stokes. Sometimes Ken would bring the gold and silver deliveries directly to us himself. Al would call me regularly and often entertain himself by making fun of Ken. For example, he would call me with Ken present and ask me if he were being unreasonable because Ken had worked there for several months and did not once prepare his coffee correctly. He said he instructed Ken to use one sugar and two creams but Ken had never gotten it right. Al would ask me,

"Am I being unreasonable or is Ken just stupid, or do you think there is something seriously wrong with him?" Al would laugh and it seemed as if he really enjoyed belittling Ken. I came to know Ken as a genuinely nice person and I felt so sorry for him. I could not understand why he would put up with Al's mean condescending attitude. I assumed he must have desperately needed the job.

I was home preparing to take our weekly supply of gold and silver to the refinery when I received a telephone call from a friend who asked, "Are you watching television?"

"No, what's up?"

He said the FBI has just made an arrest in what they say is one of the largest fencing operations on the east coast. I said I don't know anyone who would be involved in a fencing operation and I was too busy to stop working.

"I think you better turn on your television. They're showing the arrest live on every channel and I've seen this guy at your office."

My heart sank. I turned on the television and could not believe my eyes. It was Al. He was being taken out of his office in handcuffs along with his staff. They reported there had been an eight-month investigation by the Federal Bureau of Investigation and several other arrests had also been made. The reporter went on to say the thieves would actually call Al from the homes they were burglarizing and Al would tell them what to take and what not to take. The reporter then went on to say that the thieves would bring the stolen merchandise to Al and then he would fence it the next step up and there were two more arrests to be made tomorrow.

I immediately thought that the "two more" must be Sue and me. The FBI probably thinks we're part of a fencing operation. The reporter didn't say that Al would then sell the stolen goods to a legitimate wholesaler. He said, "Al fenced it the next step up."

I called Sue at the office and told her to close immediately and come directly home. On the drive home she heard the report of the arrests on the radio. She was terrified, too. Still, I reminded her how much effort we had taken to avoid anything like this from ever happening to us and assured her we had never done anything improper, let alone, participate in a fencing operation. Although, I added that we will probably be arrested tomorrow based on the reporter's comments and was absolutely confident we could prove that we had no involvement in Al's illegal operation.

I called a good friend who was a local attorney. He handled many real estate transactions for me and he lived directly across the street. He also knew Al, having handled Al's divorce. I asked him to come to my house immediately. When he arrived, I showed him the reports on television. He said this was far too big for him to handle and suggested I seek out a specialized criminal attorney to represent me.

I called Sue's dad, a retired United States Marshal, who had been in charge of the witness protection program. He knew many top criminal lawyers and recommended one. I called this lawyer, but his fees were outrageous. I told him that I didn't think I needed an attorney at this time.

The next morning Sergio asked me what to tell the FBI if they came in. I told him to tell them anything they want to know, we're not hiding anything. Shortly after we opened the office two young FBI agents arrived and asked if they could interview me. They asked me a lot of questions and I gave them honest answers. After the questioning, one of the agents said that I had a very nice office building with many separate offices, all furnished with lots of beautiful office furniture with a very expensive IBM electric typewriter on every desk; but said he didn't see anybody typing.

"We seldom have a need for a typewriter."

"Then why do you have so many? They are very expensive."

"Some people collect stamps, some pocket watches, I collect typewriters," but quickly added "I'm just kidding."

I said I was just trying to lighten things up as they were so stiff. I told him that when I opened the office many mortgage companies were closing and I bought the entire contents of one such company very cheaply and it included the nine typewriters you see here. I added, "And it makes us look very professional, don't you think?"

Suspiciously he said, "I guess you have no objection if we get the serial numbers off of them?"

"Of course not, you can get the serial numbers off of all the equipment in the office."

They spent more than an hour recording the serial numbers of every piece of equipment in the office including copy machines, digital scales, calculators, even the kitchen appliances.

The next day I received a call requesting my voluntary appearance at the U.S. Attorney's office in Washington, D.C. I was asked to bring all my records of purchases from A.B.E., Inc., Al's company. I decided at this point I was not going to be intimidated any further and I had no need to pay a costly lawyer. I knew our business procedures had been run lawfully and we could not have operated more honestly. However, Sue and her father were insistent I bring the high priced criminal lawyer I had spoken with days earlier, so I reluctantly conceded. When I arrived with my new lawyer at the U.S. Attorney's office there was not only the United States Attorney present, but several other people in the room including two senior special agents with the FBI and an agent representing the Internal Revenue Service. Could it have been any more intimidating?

For about two hours I was interrogated about my relationship with Al. When I arrived back at the office Sue asked the attorney how things went. He responded, "You don't want to know." I thanked him and told him to send me a bill and said his services would no longer be needed.

A couple of days later an FBI agent called and asked if I would meet him at his office in Washington. The next day when I arrived at the Washington Field Office I was taken into a private room. The same two senior FBI special agents that were at the meeting with the U. S. Attorney were waiting for me. You cannot possibly imagine my relief when the first thing one of the agents said was, relax you aren't in any trouble. He told me that the investigation called "Operation Green Thumb" lasted for several months. He went on to say that Ken, Al's manager (the one Al belittled all the time) was actually an undercover FBI agent. He said that Ken's report clearly exonerated us. Al told Ken never to let Sue or I know what they were doing as we were so stupid working with the police department that we would probably turn them in. He went on to say they were impressed by the extensive help I had given our local county police over the past several months.

I was absolutely startled when they asked if I would be willing to accept a position as a confidential, high level asset of the Federal Bureau of Investigation and aggressively work cases. I was relieved and was never so flattered. Of course I agreed. I received confidentiality instructions and told I would answer directly to Donald Truman, the senior special agent in charge. I was issued an official code name and number. Now another new, very exciting adventure in my life was about to begin.

Chapter 8
Oops

SUE HAD BEEN nervously waiting for me in the reception area and was anxious to know what happened. Even before starting the car to head back to the office, she insisted I explain exactly what occurred. She was as surprised as I had been to hear the details of the eight-month investigation and shocked that Ken was actually an undercover agent. I told her of the commitment I had made with the FBI. I was concerned she would not be pleased and might be very upset. On the contrary, she was very excited. She said her father had spent his life fighting crime and she couldn't wait to get started.

At first it was pretty simple. I just continued to operate our business as usual while acquiring some new dealers that were rather seedy. Many of the purchases I made from them were later secretly picked up by an agent and I was reimbursed. Sometimes an arrest would follow, but our anonymity was always paramount to the bureau and never once was there a trail leading back to us. The first few months all of the cases we worked involved stolen merchandise.

One evening while Sue and I were watching the local news, a picture was shown of a suspect that was wanted for the murder of three children. We both recognized this man as being a former tenant of ours. Neither Sue or I could sleep that night as we discussed different plans to aid the bureau with his capture. The next morning I contacted Agent Truman and he immediately generated a new case. From my rental records, Sue easily located the suspect's mother living in a suburban area just outside of Washington. I called and told her that her son rented a house from me a couple of years earlier and did not pay his water bill. I said we paid it but my office made a mistake and overpaid the bill and we had just received a refund of $211. I told her the problem was that the refund check from the Washington Suburban Sanitary Commission was made out to her son because he was the tenant and I was entitled to the refund. I asked if he would be so kind as to sign it. She said she would call him and get back to me. That same day she called back and said she had talked to her son and he said if I would bring the check to her house the following night he would be there to sign it.

The next day I was surprised when the bureau delivered to me an actual check from the Washington Suburban Sanitary Commission made payable to the suspect and it was for the exact amount that I had specified. Agent Truman instructed me that if the suspect was there, under no circumstances was I to engage in an altercation of any kind. He said no arrests would be made that evening in order to protect my anonymity. Undercover agents would be there for my protection but I would not see them. Sue insisted she wanted to go with me as we were in this together. She at least agreed to wait in the car. When his mother answered the door, she apologized saying her son had to work late, but faithfully promised that if I would leave the check with her, she would have her son sign it and would call me later to pick it up. I thanked her for her help and left the check with her.

As I returned to my car I noticed at the end of the block a plain white van. It flashed its lights and pulled away. Naturally, we followed the van. It drove about a half a mile away and pulled into a church parking lot and drove into a dark area out of sight just behind the church. As Sue and I were turning to enter the lot, a speeding car from behind pulled around and directly in front of us causing me to stop abruptly, not allowing me to enter the lot. One of the two men inside identified himself as a bureau agent and instructed me to immediately turn around and follow them to a shopping center a few miles away. There, they explained that while on stakeout for our case it appeared to them a drug deal was going down in the white van. Sue and I had actually been following drug dealers.

The bureau maintained a 24-hour surveillance on the mother's home. Within a couple of days, the suspect did arrive and picked up the check. He was not approached in any way that night. Instead, he was followed for the next two weeks. He had changed his name and acquired new employment. He was arrested on the job and never had a clue of how he was caught.

Sue and I were so impressed with the competency in which the bureau handled this case and of the extraordinary efforts taken to protect us. On the day we were notified of his arrest Sue told me our involvement in getting this desperado off the street gave her a satisfaction and joy unlike anything she had ever experienced. I told her I felt the same. We now were anxious to get more involved with new cases and were very comfortable working with the bureau and I believed they had become comfortable in working with us.

Chapter 9
Chinatown

WE CONTINUED OPERATING our business as usual. We would buy precious metals and when thugs sold us stolen merchandise, the bureau picked it up and reimbursed us. We learned of the robbery of an upscale jewelry store in an affluent section of Washington. Because of the nature of this business and the expensive inventories that jewelry stores maintained, the entrance door was usually locked and required an employee from within to electronically open it for each individual customer. A man called one such store and scheduled an appointment to have his gold Rolex wristwatch serviced. When he arrived, the well dressed gentleman that had made the appointment was buzzed in. He then held the door open while three armed hoodlums appeared from behind and entered the store along with him. While two of the robbers gathered up the inventory, the owner was forced to lay face down on the floor behind the counter. He was shot in the back of the head as his wife watched helplessly.

The morning after the robbery, I called Agent Truman and told him I believed I could be of assistance with this case. He knew that our dealers seldom sold us expensive jewelry. He asked, "What do you think you can do?" I told him most high-end jewelry stores carry insurance policies which require a photograph of many of the expensive pieces. I requested a copy of any available such photos and in less than 24 hours he delivered them to me. Afterwards, Sue and I spent many hours frequenting antique shops and retail stores that may have purchased some of the stolen jewelry and were offering it for sale. Columbia Mall in Howard County, Maryland, hosted an antique jewelry show both inside and outside every Sunday. Sue and I scanned every dealer's showcase and finally, bingo! Both of us instantly recognized a one-of-a-kind antique ladies platinum and diamond wristwatch.

There were no cell phones in those days, but from a telephone booth I called Agent Truman at his home. Fortunately he was there. He lived in Virginia and the drive to Columbia would take about an hour and a half. He asked if we would wait and said he would drop what he was doing and leave immediately. When he arrived, Sue and I sat in the mall's food court and watched as Truman, with his small young son on his shoulders, approached the dealer and asked to see the wristwatch. The dealer told him the price of the watch was $6,000. He told the dealer he didn't have that much money on him but he could give him $500 as a deposit and bring the balance the following weekend. The dealer was pleased to make the sale.

On Monday, Truman called to congratulate me and said I should be there to watch the fireworks the coming weekend. On Sunday, Sue and I were again sitting in the eatery. The mall was crowded and shoppers watched in stunned amazement as armed bureau agents approached from every direction and swarmed the booth. As the dealer was apprehended and the jewelry confiscated, his wife told the agents, "I don't know this man, he just asked me today to work for him."

I believe the bureau now realized our level of commitment and because we were willing and anxious to work cases, we could be a much greater asset to them than they had originally anticipated. Soon we began to actively work all sorts of cases.

It wasn't long before there was another major jewelry robbery in Washington. This time it was an internationally known, very high end retail establishment. The heist contained inventory valued at several million dollars. The bureau acquired information that the jewelry had been sold to a dealer in Los Angeles. They had his name and address but they needed someone to make an attempt to purchase the merchandise. Truman asked if I would. Sue and I were nervous, yet thrilled to accept. The next day I called the dealer in California. I gave him my name and the name of my company and told him I had information he had something I would like to purchase and described what I was looking for. I told him I had been in the business for over 20 years and I had a lot of contacts and it didn't matter how I knew it; I believed he had what I wanted. I told him he wanted to sell it and I had the cash to buy it. He could easily check me out. I said there was nothing for him to worry about and assured him I would pay top dollar while seeing to it that all of the merchandise was sold outside of the United States.

He said, "I don't know what you're talking about, but I could probably locate what you want." He asked if I would be willing to meet with him. Sue and I were off to beautiful Los Angeles.

He was operating out of an old office building in the jewelry district, but it was in the very low end section, just off Hill Street. Many of the stores on the block were vacant and closed. There weren't many people in the area and we wondered how many of them were local bureau agents assigned to this case. We entered an old, tiny elevator that shook from side to side as it reached his floor. It really was like something out of the movie "Chinatown." But this was not a movie, it was real and quite scary, especially when we found that he was the only tenant on his floor. We met with two middle-aged men for about 45 minutes. They never admitted they had the merchandise, but I think I made them feel secure enough to conduct the transaction with us because they assured me they could locate what I wanted and we could make the deal.

We left and went directly to an area where there were several open telephone booths in order to report directly to Truman in Washington. To make things even more interesting, there was a man at the booths telling people if they would give him a dollar he would make their call for them to anywhere in the United States and they could talk as long as they liked. I thought this was quite interesting and so I gave him a dollar. He asked me to give him the number because he had to make the call with his special credit number. I didn't give him Truman's private number, but rather the main number for the bureau. He held the phone to make sure the call went through and heard the other end answer "Federal Bureau of Investigation." He dropped the phone and ran away. After what we had just experienced, Sue and I actually needed a little levity. We reported to Truman and flew home.

As prices of gold and silver continued to fall the precious metal business slowed rapidly. We closed our office in January 1982, and moved our operation back into our home. This afforded Sue and I more time to devote to cases other than ones involving stolen property. We continued to work on stolen property cases with Truman, but he now instructed us to begin operating with other agents from the Washington, Baltimore and Frederick offices on a variety of different types of cases. There were a few cases in which rewards were offered, but we never accepted any of them and we paid all of our own expenses. Truman oversaw and was involved with every case we worked and I answered only to him. Sue and I had developed a special relationship and friendship with him. He was the most dedicated and competent law enforcement agent we had ever worked with. We could not have had more admiration or respect for him and always felt secure when he was in charge.

On one occasion Sue and I arranged a "drugs for guns exchange." The undercover bureau agent, working closely with an ATF agent, was to deliver the guns in exchange for drugs. The purchasers had made arrangements to sell the guns illegally outside of the United States, but, unfortunately for the lawbreakers, things did not go quite as they planned.

On another occasion I was informed of a local state senator that was taking bribes for special political favors. I arranged to meet with the senator along with an undercover bureau agent posing as my partner and give him $15,000 in exchange for his support for our fabricated request. The case did not go as easily as we hoped, but ultimately he was charged and convicted.

It wasn't long before new cases were opened with information solely provided by Sue and me. Truman preferred we not work on cases involving drug dealers. Although he worked these cases, he considered it far too dangerous for us. However, I was working undercover with some pretty seedy characters, one of which bragged to me that he knew a high level drug criminal that was out on bond awaiting trial. I not only secured the offender's name, I also learned he planned to leave the country the following night with several million dollars in cash which was stored in a secret vault behind his home. As a result of the information I provided to Truman, the criminal was apprehended along with the money shortly before his planned departure.

A friend and acquaintance complained to me he had performed work for a businessman who refused to pay him what he called a lousy $50,000. He said the businessman was extremely wealthy and had purchased for himself and his friends several multi-million-dollar-homes in his area. He asked me if I would help him get the money that was owed to him. I agreed to go with my friend to a local shopping center where the man owned and operated a small retail store. He was rather pleasant to us only because the reason given for the introduction was supposedly solely for the possibility of my doing business with him. When we left, I asked my friend what other businesses this entrepreneur owned.

"None that I know of."

"That doesn't make sense, you tell me this man is a multi-millionaire. Where did he get his money?" I asked him what more he knew about this person.

He said only that he had been recently divorced in a neighboring county. I told him divorce records are usually open to the public as long as children were not involved and he could possibly gather a wealth of information from those records.

A few days later, he was very excited when he called and told me he acquired the transcripts of the man's divorce hearing. The transcripts revealed the man testified that he never had an inheritance of any kind. He also testified his income never exceeded $100,000 a year. My friend said, "You were right, he must have an illegal operation somewhere. I'm going to tell him if he doesn't give me my money I'm going to report him to the IRS."

I telephoned this information to Truman. Inasmuch as all of this transpired outside of his jurisdiction and in another state, he relayed what I had told him to the local FBI office. When Truman called back, he said the agent in the suspect's state told him that if this person was doing activities that would generate that kind of illegal funds, they certainly would know about it. Yet, as a result of Truman's insistence, he agreed to open a case and start an investigation. A few months later, several major newspapers throughout the country and many major national magazines carried the story of the arrest and seizure of tens of millions of dollars in cash and real estate including yachts and jet airplanes owned by this one man. The court ordered him to pay restitution of almost $80 million to his victims and he was sentenced to more than 35 years in prison.

Almost never did Sue or I feel that we were in any danger. I say almost never because sometimes it just couldn't be avoided. We had been working a real scoundrel who had a smorgasbord of illicit activities. He was selling drugs to students at local junior high schools on a regular basis. We became involved because he was also dealing heavily in stolen property. He even arranged for a teenager to work at a local retirement home in Baltimore and taught him how to get into the residents' safety deposit boxes and bring him the contents. He would then sell us the stolen property. He was as low as anyone could possibly be. We were always nervous dealing with him as he too used drugs which made him extremely erratic. Sometimes his behavior was okay, but sometimes he was very nasty and on a couple of occasions, he even became a little violent. Making things worse, he would never come to my office, but always to my home and always at night. After selling me the stolen property, the bureau would pick it up the following morning to build their case and ultimately have the property returned to the proper owners.

He called one afternoon and said he was coming over that evening. He sounded like he was very high and I didn't feel like dealing with him that night as we already had had an exhausting day. I told him that Sue and I would not be home that night and he could come by first thing in the morning. He told me he didn't care what time I got home and said he needed to come over that night. I told him he didn't understand; Sue and I would be out all night and wouldn't be returning home until about ten o'clock the next morning. He seemed agitated but said he would just come by in the morning.

Before going to sleep that night I notified the agent working this case with us, Agent Davis (out of the Baltimore office) and Truman of the situation. About two o'clock in the morning I heard noises outside. With the lights out, I quietly walked down a hallway and entered a guest bedroom where I had a good view of our front entrance. There he was trying to pick the lock on my front door and with him was a large seedy looking man I had never seen before. I ran for my loaded 12-gauge shotgun that was in my bedroom. I sat about halfway down our staircase giving me a full view of the double-door entry they were trying to break into. Sue called Davis at his home and notified him of the situation. He immediately wanted to call the county police and Sue agreed with him. I, however, insisted I was sure they could not enter my home as I had installed the best double-bolt locking systems available as well as an extremely good security system. I knew if the police caught him in the act of trying to break into my home it could seriously jeopardize the many months spent on the investigation. As I sat on the stairway with my shotgun pointed at the front doors, Sue stayed on the phone with Davis reporting everything minute-by-minute what was happening. After trying to pick the lock for a little over an hour, they got back in their car and sat smoking cigarettes, or whatever. I thought they were going to leave, but after their short break they got out of the car and tried the lock for about another hour. With no success they finally left.

Agent Davis stayed on the telephone during the entire episode and for about half an hour afterwards. The next morning, the dealer came by and we did business as usual as if nothing ever happened. It wasn't long before he was arrested and charged with a variety of crimes and received a very long prison sentence. Sue and I were relieved.

Most of the cases we worked were really not very dangerous except for a few I am unable to talk about. Any small risk we did take was far outweighed by the overwhelming rewards gained by helping to take off the streets criminals who, rather than work, enriched themselves at the expense of honest, hard-working people without any regard for the pain and suffering they inflicted. Few people have more disdain for these selfish thugs than Sue and I. To this day even most of our closest friends have no idea of our participation with law enforcement and we have never regretted our contribution. In fact, we are very appreciative of the opportunities we were given and if I weren't so darn old I'd love to do it again.

Chapter 10
If It Sounds Too Good To Be True …

ALTOGETHER, WORKING WITH the original county police detectives and the federal agents, we were involved with more than 100 cases over the course of almost 20 years. Now that you have some idea of the variety of cases we worked, let me tell you about one more case that was the most gratifying of all.

My sister JoAnne and her husband Mike, live in Toronto, Canada. He is a CPA and worked for a small insurance company. She was very excited when she called to tell me the company her husband worked for was expanding and the owner had offered him a partnership position. She said this was made possible because their broker in Toronto secured a loan for the company in the amount of $5 million. I asked what the company's assets were and what security they had pledged. She said they had not pledged any securities at all and their assets were very small. I was puzzled and asked why any investor would give such a loan. She told me I did not understand the nature of the business and the company had promised the investor a position on the board. I told her it didn't make any sense to me and to just be careful. Above all, don't let Mike invest any of his savings, I advised. She laughed and said her broker told her the investor's company lends hundreds of millions of dollars and assured her the investor would not ask for any fees or funds of any kind. Mr. Grimm represented the investors and he flew to Canada to meet with them.

After seeing their small office located in a very modest area of Toronto, he told them this was not acceptable. He said he could only be involved and make the loan if they would relocate the office into a much larger space. It had to be in a building located in one of the most exclusive areas in Toronto. They were concerned about the increased cost, but Grimm assured them he would be sending them a sizable number of new elite clients who only dealt with the most prestigious of firms. He was going to teach them how to become extremely successful as he had done for others.

I became even more concerned when my sister told me he said that the loan was committed and would be dispersed as soon as they were set up in their new office. I suggested she get a commitment in writing. After receiving the commitment in writing, the woman who owned the insurance company used her personal funds to meet his request. Grimm raised the commitment to $10 million and said he was pleased to help them become one of Toronto's most successful insurance companies.

Soon, Grimm was sending clients to their office requesting some very unusual insurance policies. One of the policies insured an oil tanker shipment and another a large transfer of gold bullion. They fulfilled his requests, but instead of the funds from the loan, they received only more assurances that the money was being transferred. Their expenses were soaring and after only a few months the owner of the insurance company had exhausted her savings. They had many assurances the money would arrive at any time including a letter from a bank in France confirming the money was there and in the process of being transferred.

The owner offered Mike a 15 percent stake in the company for a large contribution the company needed until the funds for the loan arrived. He agreed and invested his life savings. Other employees agreed to work without receiving a paycheck until the funds arrived.

My sister, now panicking, was calling me almost every day. Grimm kept insisting there was no need to worry; it was just taking a little longer than he thought it would. Finally, they told Grimm they were months behind on their rent and the landlord was coming with law enforcement to padlock the office in just a few days. My sister was relieved when she called and said the money had been wired and Grimm said they would receive it by the end of that business day.

The money never came, the office was padlocked and closed, and the owner and my sister lost everything. My sister was crying when she asked "Why would he do this to us? Mr. Grimm never asked for any money or anything else. What motive could he have possibly had?" Up until now she refused to tell me his name or give me any information about him. She was concerned I might interfere; now there was no reason not to.

I waited about a week before calling Grimm. When I did, I introduced myself and told him the name of my company. I said I was returning his call and asked him what he wanted. He was very polite and said, "I don't remember calling you." I told him he had called my company a couple of weeks ago and asked for Timothy Rogers, a name I just invented. I said Mr. Rogers was out of town on business and asked me to return the call. Again he insisted he didn't remember calling and asked me what kind of business I was in. I spoke very fast to give him the impression I was very busy. I told him I didn't have time for games and asked if he was trying to sell us something. He continued to insist that he couldn't remember why he called. Thinking I could entice him into trying to get money out of me I told him I was a commercial lender and asked him if he were possibly looking for a loan. He laughed and said, "I'm a billionaire, I have no need to borrow money, I can't spend what I have." I gave him my telephone number and said that if he had a change of heart to please call me. I felt certain he would call me back, but he didn't.

About two weeks later, I called him and apologized for being so short and rude a couple of weeks earlier. I told him I was thinking about what he said and that I was very impressed. I didn't know any billionaires. I was just a struggling young businessman and asked if he would mind telling me how he made all his money. He was very talkative and told me of his involvement in several different businesses. He often ended the conversation by mentioning a specific activity he and his wife were involved with at their church. This conversation lasted for about two hours. I called Truman and reported what I was doing and that I believed this man was a professional confidence artist. I explained what he had done to my sister and that he probably had many other victims in the United States as his office was located in the Midwest. Truman told me if I learned any such actual information, he would open a case. Over the next few months, I developed a great relationship with Grimm usually speaking on the telephone with him more than once a week. It was obvious he enjoyed telling me about the sophisticated deals he was doing and boasting about how much money he was making.

Ironically, one evening I was having dinner with one of my closest friends, Alan, who told me of the great deal he had just gotten into in California. He invested several hundred thousand dollars in a multi-million dollar gold bullion transfer investment. He had been promised a 24 percent return in six months. I asked him how he knew the gold bullion or the transfer actually existed. "Aren't you afraid of losing that kind of money?"

He said, "I'm not stupid. I wouldn't invest that kind of money without really checking it out well."

I asked him how he checked it out.

First of all he said, "The entire transfer is completely insured. I have a policy guaranteeing me that if anything happens during the transfer, I will be fully reimbursed." Of course he said, "I won't make my 24 percent if that happens, but I won't lose any money."

I asked him what he knew about the insurance company that was guaranteeing his funds. He told me because his investment was so large, he flew to Massachusetts where the insurance company offices were located and he could see that everything was on the up and up and felt very secure about his investment.

It was too late for me to help my friend, but at least I now knew the scam. Another unsuspecting insurance company would also go down and their policies would be worthless. I couldn't wait to tell Truman and called him at his home that night. In the morning he opened a case.

I continued to have conversations with Grimm, my new so-called billionaire friend. At one point I asked him if I could arrange a loan of a couple million dollars for him so I could make a few bucks. He told me he loved our conversations and had grown very fond of me. He said he would like to help me, but a couple of million to him was far too small of an amount for him to waste his time. I asked how much I would need to have before he wouldn't be "wasting his time." He said at least $50 million. I told him there was no way I could ever have that kind of money available. He chuckled and said, "Well if you ever do, you have my number."

Our conversations continued over the next several weeks. Truman's investigation revealed there was an entire network of these high level confidence men operating throughout the United States and they were all working together.

I told my friend Alan I had read an article in the newspaper reporting there were lots of confidence games going on at high levels. Without telling him anything about what I was doing, I tried my best to inform him of these confidence schemes. Unfortunately, he refused to listen or believe a con man could swindle him. He insisted these were not con men. He said last month they called him with a second opportunity and said this would be a quick in-and-out deal and he could double his money very quickly. It was only $25,000 which he gave them and just that day, he received a check from them for $50,000. He said it was the easiest money he ever made.

He told me of a third deal he had just gotten into. He said this time he didn't have enough money, but the deal was so good he borrowed it by posting his home as collateral. He had also put up several hundred thousand dollars on this deal. This time it was for oil. He explained when oil is shipped, the tankers are never completely full and it is possible to safely put an additional 10 percent aboard. Because Japan was in such dire need of petroleum they would be willing to pay a premium for this oil. Once again he was promised a 24 percent return in six months and again his investment was insured. The most he said he could lose was the interest it cost him to borrow the money and that was such a small amount compared to the opportunity of easily making so much money.

I couldn't believe my ears. I thought my friend was quite bright; these confidence men were really good. I felt so incredibly bad for him and literally begged him not to do any more of these investments. He told me I was just jealous because I wasn't in on the deal.

By now Truman had learned of several other victims. One was an 80 year-old American citizen living in the Cayman Islands. She had a business there most of her life but now wanted to retire and move back to the United States. She managed to save $3 million and counseled with the broker on the island about getting it legally in the U.S. without having to pay taxes. Somehow, she was introduced to this group who told her to give them the money and they would invest it and return it to her tax free when she arrived in America. She, of course, never saw her money again. Another victim was taken for $6 million. Unbelievably, he was a United States Congressman's son. The list of victims seemed endless. I was now more determined than ever to bring these ruthless miscreants to justice and so was the FBI.

My telephone friendship with Grimm had developed over the course of several months and by now I believed he really trusted me and was ready to reel me in. I called him acting very excited and told him I had just left a meeting with a large medical group that had invested small amounts with me in the past. It had only been a few million dollars before, but now they were willing to give me their entire retirement fund amounting to just over $50 million. He remained calm and told me he really didn't need the money, but knowing I had worked so hard and he had developed such a fondness for me he would take the loan on one condition, that he would not pay anything over the prime rate of interest. To make the deal appear legitimate, I told him they wanted one point above prime. He said he would have to refuse the loan. I told him I didn't think I could get them to agree to reduce their rate, but I would get back to him in a day or two. I didn't call him back for about a week thinking he would call me. Surprisingly, he didn't; this guy was really good.

When I did call him back I told him I had gotten them to agree to the prime rate of interest because of the large quantity of assets he told me he was willing to pledge. I told him I had spent a lot of time in arranging this and had gotten him an incredibly good rate. I asked him how much money he was going to pay me.

"I have never paid to secure a loan, but because of our special friendship I'll agree to give you one-quarter of a percent. But, I must make the payment with gold bullion which comes directly from my refineries."

I told him how much I appreciated him doing this for me. He said it's just the beginning and that we were going to do lots of deals together. I told him it would only take a couple of weeks to have the paperwork prepared. "The only thing I need to do is have you pledge the assets you told me about." He said he would overnight me all the information.

The next day I received a very professional looking prospectus provided by a law firm containing about 300 pages outlining his assets in detail.

There were copies of securities and bearer bonds with valid cusip numbers totaling over $100 million. Also, there were documents from the leading private security warehouse in the United States known as the "Fort Knox for the private sector," certifying that they were storing several tons of ore for him in 55 gallon drums. Receipts confirming payment for the storage amounting to thousands of dollars per month were also provided. Detailed assays of the ore from one of the nation's leading refineries were included in the prospectus. To top it all off there was a complete asset value report from one of the country's top accounting firms. They used the quantities and weights provided them by the security company, as well as the assays provided by the major refinery, to calculate the total value of gold, silver and palladium contained within the ore. It was valued at somewhat over $1 billion dollars.

It all looked legitimate and was extremely convincing. I think the bureau became a little nervous after verifying the ore was actually stored at that warehouse. I assured them that those drums were filled with sand and although the security certificates and cusip numbers checked out as legitimate, I believed that they must be counterfeit. I concluded the refinery had simply been furnished ore samples that were not actually taken from those drums. The well-respected accounting firm simply used the figures provided by the refinery and the weights provided by the security company to compute the value. The security company, the refinery and the accounting firm were unaware of the illegal activities. The scheme was brilliant.

I called Grimm and told him I met with the medical group and they were very pleased with the prospectus and authorized me to transfer the $52 million to the main office of a major national bank in Washington. I told him I was having the appropriate collateral documents prepared and I arranged a meeting for the coming Friday at the bank for Grimm to sign the documents and receive the funds by certified check. I told Truman that Sue had also spent many hours talking with this man and wanted to attend the meeting. He had no objection.

On Thursday I picked up Grimm at Washington National Airport and introduced Truman as my partner "Timothy Rogers." He said he was thrilled to finally meet us in person. I'm sure he was impressed as I was driving a new Rolls Royce. We headed directly to a nearby restaurant where we enjoyed some really good conversation with him. Grimm could not have more strongly expressed the fondness he had developed for Sue and me, to my partner, Truman. He said he wanted to help me make really big money and he had something to talk to me about tomorrow after the bank meeting. He said it was easy making the money, but to keep it you had to be very careful because the government was always trying to get you.

I said, "Do you mean the IRS?"

"No, they're no problem. I can show you how to have all of your earnings overseas so the IRS can never touch you. It's the FBI. They're the problem and they are everywhere, and when you make really big money they are always after you."

"Oh my gosh, are there any in here?"

"No, I checked the place out."

"How do you know?"

"I can smell them."

I looked over at Sue. She was literally biting her lip to prevent from busting out laughing. I didn't know it at the time, but later learned there were other undercover agents working this case in the same restaurant. After lunch we dropped Grimm off at his hotel.

The next morning we met in a private office at the bank. There were employees facilitating the transaction so that all the agreements posting the securities for collateral and consummating liens on the ore in the security warehouse were done properly. Again, unknown to me at the time, all the so-called bank employees at this meeting were undercover agents of the bureau. Clearly visible on the conference table was the certified check made payable to him for the full amount, $52 million. After completion of the signing of all the documents, the bank officer said that because it was past two o'clock and Monday being a holiday, the check would be sent overnight and delivered to him on Tuesday. He assured Grimm the interest charged for the three days that Grimm wouldn't have the money would be paid to him with a separate check. Grimm was satisfied with that arrangement.

Before taking Grimm back to the airport he reminded me again that he had something he wanted to talk to me about. He said he was so impressed with Sue and me that he wanted to do something very special for us. He produced another prospectus on a project he claimed he just received. He said he purchased the rights to a closed down gold mine. The prospectus contained geological reports showing the mine had been closed in 1935 when gold was only $35 an ounce and at that time the cost of mining exceeded the value of the gold. Now, with new technology and the soaring price of gold, it would become extremely profitable to reopen the mine and he purchased the rights for $4 million.

Grimm said to honor his promise to see that Sue and I made an incredible amount of money he was willing to take me in as a full partner on this deal. I said that may not be a lot of money to you but if this deal went bad I would lose everything I owned as $2 million was all the money I had and could borrow. In being so generous to us he personally guaranteed my half so that it would be impossible for me to lose any money at all.

I told him I trusted him immensely and as I pulled out my checkbook and was in the process of writing him a check for $2 million, Truman asked him how much money we could make off of this deal. He responded, "It's in the B's." I acted as if I was very excited. Truman being the cautious soul that he is said, "I'll take this check back to the bank and have it delivered to you along with the bank check on Tuesday." Everyone seemed pleased.

Can you imagine the level of scum we were dealing with? He genuinely believed on Tuesday he was going to be receiving a check for $52 million and yet he was not only willing, but anxious, to get every last penny Sue and I had and financially destroy us.

On Tuesday morning the delivery man, who in reality was a bureau agent, arrested him as he accepted the package. The next day he posted bond and called me. I said to him, "What the hell is going on? The FBI raided my house and took all of my records!"

Without mentioning his arrest he said, "It's all a big mistake and I'll have it cleared up by the end of the week. The important thing is we don't lose this gold mine deal. Do you still have the $2 million in the bank?"

I told him of course I did and he asked me if I could wire it to him. I made him grovel a little convincing me that there was nothing to worry about, but finally agreed to go to the bank and wire him the money. That night when he called I told him I had been very busy, but would certainly do it first thing in the morning.

He called every day for about a week and every day I assured him I would be sending the money. Finally, I told him I had received a call from a woman that claimed she owned an insurance company and told me how he had financially destroyed her. His exact words were, "Don't believe her, she's the devil on wheels." I told him I was just too afraid to deal with him anymore, but to call me as soon as he got his situation resolved and I would be glad to discuss possible future arrangements.

He was found guilty and received a very long prison sentence. There was no sand in the fifty-five gallon drums; it was actually all fine gravel and I was told the security storage company used it for a driveway.

As for my naïve good friend who had invested more than a million dollars; he called me a few weeks later in an absolute panic and said he received a call from an FBI agent in California who told him he had been scammed. All of his money was gone. I could only tell him how truly sorry I was.

I never told my sister what I was doing until after the sentencing. Unfortunately I couldn't erase the pain she suffered, or the pain of my very close friend, but at least these unscrupulous criminals wouldn't be victimizing anyone else for a very long time.

Chapter 11
Don't Mess With The IRS

WORKING CASES WITH the bureau actually consumed a very small amount of our overall time which we now had more of after closing the precious metals office. Other than the short break I took years earlier, after closing my real estate office in the mid-70s, I had worked long hours every day for so many years it had become part of my DNA and I had no plans to slow down now.

Although the precious metal business boom was pretty much over, the bad economy provided some really great new opportunities. I believed an economic recovery was just around the corner and these opportunities could soon be gone just as quickly as was the precious metal business. I did what I knew best, invested in real estate, and continued to spend a good amount of my time purchasing new properties to add to my real estate rental portfolio.

The bad economy provided other great opportunities as well. When the economy goes south usually the first thing people stop purchasing are luxury items. Jewelry stores were among the hardest hit retail establishments. Through our gemology training, Sue and I acquired enough knowledge to take advantage of this. Jewelry stores were closing everywhere and often the inventory was sold by their creditors. We flew around the country purchasing part, or sometimes all, of the stock of many of these stores. Usually they were offered by closed bid. We would simply get a list of the inventory and offer about 10 to 15 percent of the original jewelry store owner's wholesale cost. Most of our bids were rejected as being lower than the creditors were willing to accept. However, enough were accepted so that within a couple of years we had purchased several million dollars worth of jewelry inventory.

At the time I had no idea what I was going to do with it, but I did know it was a great investment and we were having the time of our lives. My thought was when the economy recovered maybe we would open up a jewelry store in a mall. We certainly had accumulated enough inventory and Sue and I very much enjoyed dealing with the jewelry and gemstones. It was a lot more fun than anything else we were doing to make money and it had the potential of earning a good amount of additional income.

Sometimes at these creditors sales there were items offered other than jewelry. At one sale there was a Triumph motorcycle put up for bid. I had absolutely no interest in purchasing a motorcycle, especially one as big and heavy as this one and apparently neither did anyone else. At the time the Triumph had a retail value of about $5,000 and the creditor's auctioneer was trying to get $3,000. As nobody was bidding the auctioneer kept lowering the bid and when he reached $800 I raised my hand. "Sold!" he shouted. I couldn't pass up a bargain like this. The location of the sale was very close to our home and the auctioneer agreed to deliver the motorcycle to my house. Sue was not happy I purchased the motorcycle and insisted, if I kept it, I would make her a widow. She made me promise to sell it immediately. As soon as we got home even before the auctioneer dropped off the motorcycle she placed an ad in the classified section of the newspaper advertising it for sale.

The very next day I had the motorcycle in my circular driveway directly in front of my home. I was wearing old ratty clothes I only wore when I was doing very dirty work around the house. I had no shoes or socks on as I cleaned and polished the motorcycle, preparing it for sale. I looked awful, but I wasn't expecting anyone. I had a view of our other driveway leading into our garage from an adjacent street. A car pulled into that driveway with a woman who looked to be in her early 20s accompanied by a much older man. The house directly across from my driveway was for sale and often real estate salesmen I knew would park in my driveway while they showed that house. I didn't know these people and I thought it quite nervy of them. It was a little intimidating and I was embarrassed about my ghastly attire. I started the motorcycle and drove across my front lawn to their car and loudly asked, "Can I help you?" Both of them jumped out of their car, held identification and badges high into the air and I think they identified themselves as Treasury Department agents. I remember asking them if they were with the Internal Revenue Service. They said yes and asked, "Are you Edward Primoff?"

"Yes I am; put those badges away before you scare all my neighbors to death. If you want to talk to me come into the house."

I raced into the house making sure to talk to Sue before she was unsuspectingly surprised by them. Sue was cleaning out the refrigerator and had its contents spread on all the countertops and kitchen table, making the kitchen a real mess. I told her there were two agents from the IRS that would be entering our house in a moment and they wanted to talk to us. With a startled look on her face Sue said, "That's not funny." With that the doorbell rang and I let them in.

The woman agent said, "Mr. Primoff you have the right to remain silent; you have the right to an attorney."

I stopped her and chuckled a little, "You're giving me my Miranda rights?"

"Yes, let me finish."

"I don't need an attorney; ask me anything you want."

She told me I had the right to stop the interview at any time. Again I told her to just ask me anything she wanted. She said, "All right, there are rumors, and at this point they are just rumors, that you purchased hundreds of thousands of dollars in precious metals and paid everyone with cash."

Sounding a little angry I responded, "That's a vicious, ugly rumor."

"I thought you'd say that."

"It was millions of dollars." I looked over at Sue, she had a lump in her throat and was flush; it looked to me as if she might pass out.

The IRS agent told me I didn't have to make these admissions and could stop the interview at any time and still get an attorney. I asked her why in the world I would need an attorney. She asked "Well, why did you pay everybody with cash?" I told her the IRS regulations did not forbid me from paying with cash for my precious metal purchases. Before I started this business, I called the Internal Revenue Service to confirm that my understanding of the law was correct and was told it absolutely was; there was no regulation restricting me from paying for my purchases with cash. The IRS employee I had spoken with told me I could pay with cash, but strongly advised me to keep good records. She puzzlingly asked, "But why would you pay everybody with cash?"

I took a dollar out my pocket and read directly off the bill, "This note is legal tender for all debts, public and private. When people give me their precious metals, I have a debt to them so I paid it with cash." Again I reminded her, there is no law or IRS regulation prohibiting it.

She arrogantly asked, "I guess you have receipts?"

I said of course I do, I have receipts for every dollar I spent. She asked if they could see them. I told her I did not keep the records at my home as the volume of boxes containing them was so massive, I owned and maintained a separate warehouse solely for their storage. I told her it would take several truckloads to bring them to my house.

She asked how soon I could do that as they wanted to review all the records. I told her that would be a problem as I had been actively working for the Federal Bureau of Investigation and many of the receipts are confidential and I am not at liberty to disclose them. It's difficult to describe their demeanor or the expressions on their faces; but both of the agents looked at each other as if they knew they were dealing with a crazy loon who had fabricated a wild and ridiculous excuse trying to avoid showing them anything. I believe they were certain I didn't have any records at all just like many of the gold buying dealers they had recently investigated.

The woman said, "Of course you realize we are going to have to confirm all of this with the FBI."

"By all means, let me help you." I picked up my telephone and dialed my direct line to Truman and handed her the phone. Truman instructed her to leave my house immediately and have her supervisor deal directly with his office. Although Sue did not agree, I thought it was kind of a fun experience.

A couple days later Truman called and told me that the bureau was taking the position they did not want any of my records reviewed by the Internal Revenue Service as they still had several open cases contained within those files. I strongly objected. I told Truman I was afraid if I didn't show my records to the IRS they would assume I didn't really have them and I had just been jerking them around. The last thing I needed was to become an enemy of the Internal Revenue Service. I thought how very unfair that would be, especially because I had kept such copious records and paid income tax on every single dollar I made. I was proud of that and wanted the IRS to be assured that I sought a full and complete audit. Truman told me he understood my concern. He had a meeting scheduled with the Internal Revenue Service supervisors and would try to work out something that would be satisfactory to everyone and said he would get back to me.

When he called back a few days later, agent Truman told me he thought I would be happy with the agreement he reached with the Internal Revenue Service. The audit was to be permitted with the condition that the IRS could only use the information gathered through my records to assure themselves that I had reported and paid income tax on every single transaction. Any other information they acquired and intended to use had to be cleared through the bureau. He also told me he made it abundantly clear to them that I was extremely anxious and agreeable for the audit to go forth.

The same two IRS agents that originally came to my house now returned for a full review of my records. It appeared to me, by the young lady's attitude, that she was not very happy with the arrangement her supervisors made with the bureau. She remained socially frigid the entire time she spent with us. Sue and I couldn't imagine that she had anything personally against us and believed she must have just resented all business people. However, the older agent seemed as if he had no concern with the agreement and just wanted to get on with the audit of our records. He was very professional and exhibited no animosity toward us. I took them into my office where I had placed dozens of boxes of our records and receipts. They were well organized with the preceding year's records and transactions. Sue offered them coffee and donuts but both of them refused and said it would be inappropriate. I told them they needed to lighten up a little.

The first few days they spent several hours recording their own records of each of my transactions and asking me questions about several of my receipts. They told me that they knew I was not required to get identification from the dealers I was purchasing from. They asked how I knew the person signing the receipt was actually that person and hadn't just made up a name? I told them I knew most of the dealers and knew they were using their legitimate names. I said, however, there were dealers I did not know very well and I suspected some of them were using fictitious names. There was no law or regulation requiring me to authenticate their signatures or confirm in any way that they were representing themselves legitimately. Yet, because of my concern and for my own information, I took precautions to assure myself that I could locate these people if it ever became necessary. I told the agents to look at the bottom right corner of each receipt. Some of them had letters and numbers written there. They were the car license plate numbers we recorded after the dealers left. Those receipts represented the only dealers selling to us that we didn't know. By getting the tag numbers we were assured we could locate anyone who sold us anything. I believe at that point both of the IRS agents understood how meticulously clean our business operation had been because the older agent asked if he could still get a cup of coffee and became very pleasant to work with.

The young lady's demeanor on the other hand didn't change at all. I think she was upset she couldn't find anything improper and she remained unable to conceal her resentment towards us. I say that because occasionally she would drop what I considered an inappropriate remark expressing her dissatisfaction about the unfairness of the extremely large amount of money we had made when so many others in the country were struggling.

After spending all day with them for about a week, I asked the young lady why she was always so uptight and upset. I told her she could spend as long as she wanted reviewing and dissecting our receipts and records and assured her she was not going to find anything improper. I remember telling her if I walked down the street and found 25 cents I would write it down and make sure to pay tax on it because I would rather the Mafia have a contract on my life than for the IRS to think I cheated them out of 25 cents; at least I would have a chance with the Mafia. The older man laughed heartily; but the young agent always remained expressionless.

One day, while I was working with them as they were documenting and recording transactions, the phone rang and it just so happened that it was one of our old county police detective friends. I said, "I can't talk to you right now, the Gestapo's here." Again the older IRS agent laughed and the young agent was unresponsive. In the evenings after the agents left Sue would always be very upset with me for doing that sort of thing. I really was only trying to soften things a little with the young IRS agent while I readily admit to having a little fun doing it too. I think they were there between two and three weeks. Of course there was nothing found to be improper and the case was closed with no additional taxes due and no change to our tax returns.

There is one thing I would like to point out. The young IRS agent is possibly now retired. I am 70 years old and still agonizing every day with business problems. Also I had started working at least 20 years before she did. I can't help but wonder if she still has the same disdain for business people like me. I remember thinking how terrible it would be if the entire IRS Agency ever developed her attitudes and ideologies. Even worse, what if it was the entire United States Government? Of course, I was sure that could never happen.

Chapter 12
Another Totally New Unexpected Direction

RECENTLY A FRIEND, who happens to be a college professor, told me he watched several reports on television stating there were predictions thousands of years ago that the world would come to an end on December 20, 2012. He said, of course, he didn't believe them, yet it still made him a little nervous. That is similar to the way I felt in 1983. Fourteen years earlier Mayo Clinic advised me it would be very unlikely for me to live past the age of 40 and this was the year I would reach that age. That was something I lived with and thought about often. Every time I got sick or developed one of the dreaded medical conditions they predicted, especially when it resulted in excruciating pain, I could not help but wonder if I had come to the end of my road.

In 1969 they described to me in detail a litany of adverse medical conditions I was sure to develop in the coming years and many of them had already actually occurred. Fortunately, for me, medical science had stayed one step ahead with new procedures and new drugs that had been developed over the years that were not available in 1969. Most of the dire conditions that did occur were either solved or at least postponed thanks to Johns Hopkins Hospital and the incredible care I received from the chief gastroenterologist, Dr. Thomas Hendrix at that hospital.

Most fortunate of all for me was the fact that I was married to the most wonderfully optimistic woman in the world. Sue always suggested we continue working and insisted we remain active in all the projects we were involved with. She often would say I had more energy than anyone else she knew and I was going to live to be 100. Her reassuring words often made me feel she was possibly right. Therefore, I just kept pushing forward and wondering what kind of crazy thing would happen next.

I did not have to wonder very long before sure enough something crazy did happen. One of my closest friends, Peter Scop, who happened to be a senior analyst working for the Defense Intelligence Agency, called to tell me of a good opportunity. I had a great amount of respect both for his character and his intelligence. He had a doctorate degree in nuclear physics; he wasn't just smart, he was truly brilliant. I was a little surprised when he told me he had a small lending business and had been investing in some commercial loans. He said he had a request for a really good loan, but was currently low on funds and suggested I loan the borrower the money he needed. I asked him if it was risky. He told me if he thought these loans were risky he wouldn't be doing them himself and certainly wouldn't be suggesting them to me. I asked him to tell me about this loan. He said the borrower was a builder who paid $50,000 for a building lot he now owned free and clear and wanted a loan in the amount of $125,000 to construct a single-family home on the property. After the construction was complete he intended to sell the home for $250,000. "I guess the builder has really good credit for you to consider this loan?"

"I don't run credit reports, they usually only depress me." he said.

"Why would you even consider this loan? What if the builder never builds a house on the lot?" He said let me finish and then told me in addition to the lot the builder was also going to secure the loan with his personal residence he was currently living in, which appraised at $450,000.

"What interest rate is he willing to pay?" The rate was about six percent higher than it would cost me to borrow the money from the bank and almost 10 percent more than the interest I was getting from money I already had in my savings account. Of course I said I'd make the loan with that amount of collateral.

I asked Peter if there were a good number of this type of commercial loans available with this much equity.

"Probably more than you can handle." He told me there were many small business people who had good collateral and needed to borrow money for one reason or another but couldn't get, or wait, for bank approval. They were willing to pay somewhat higher than bank rates. Over the past 15 years, I had purchased hundreds of homes and three office buildings. Both Sue and I had taken, and passed, real estate appraisal courses given at our local university. We also successfully completed real estate classes and seminars given by the Society of Real Estate Appraisers. I had been adjudicated as an expert witness and personally testified as to real estate values in three different jurisdictions. I was confident that there were few people who knew the real estate business any better than me. I was as qualified as anyone, if not more so, to be in the commercial lending business. I knew I could take full advantage of all of the real estate expertise I had acquired and was anxious and excited to seize this great new opportunity.

It was 1984 and real estate values were finally rapidly rising again. I decided to sell all of our rental and investment properties and invest the profits into our new commercial loan business. As quickly as disbursements from individual sales were received, they were lent out on good commercial loans, always secured with real estate of a much higher value than the face value of our loan. We never advertised to acquire any of these loans as we were receiving loan requests regularly from attorneys, accountants and loan brokers.

By the middle of 1985, all of our rentals and investment properties had been sold and every dollar was invested into our new lending business. We were out of properties to sell and out of money to lend, but we were still receiving requests for what we considered to be high quality loans and I didn't want to turn them down. I needed money and a lot of it. I had borrowed hundreds of thousands of dollars for my business from a national bank that I had been dealing with for several years, but I was skeptical of how they would react to a request that my line of credit be raised several million dollars.

At an arranged meeting, I explained to the bank officers what I was doing and showed them the profits I was making. They were even more impressed than I thought they would be. They approved a line of credit for several million dollars. The only requirement was that they would only loan me 70 percent of the face value of each note. That meant I had to have 30 percent invested myself and of course they would hold my notes as security for the line of credit. This was really great as it raised my lending power to almost $10 million and in 1985 that was a whole lot of money.

Chapter 13
Final Straw

WITH MY AVERAGE loan being usually somewhere between $250,000 and $500,000 it didn't take me long to realize even this large amount of money could quickly be exhausted. The commercial loans I made were about five percent higher than the rate I was paying to borrow the money on my line of credit. That meant for every million dollars I borrowed from the bank and loaned out in commercial loans I earned $50,000. I also knew it would be very advantageous for me to raise more capital as the bank was requiring me to have 30 percent of my own money in each loan.

The answer was obvious. I had dozens of large safety deposit boxes filled with the jewelry I purchased just a few years earlier when the economy had tanked. The country was doing much better now and it was a good time to sell the entire inventory of jewelry. My idea was to open a jewelry store in a popular mall. We certainly had enough inventory to fully stock a retail site several times over. Sue was very much against opening any retail establishment because she thought it would consume far too much of our time and argued we needed to focus our efforts on our new lending business. She also reminded me that we still had responsibilities on the cases we were working for the bureau and neither one of us wanted to give that up.

A very close friend of mine, Arnold Duke, was the co-owner of the International Gem and Jewelry Show Company. He suggested I liquidate my inventory at his shows. The shows were only on Friday, Saturday and

Sunday, so it wouldn't take much time away from our lending business. I told him I didn't think I could do it. I believed the pain and the medical problems I was experiencing would prevent me from being able to stand on my feet behind a booth 10 hours a day waiting on customers. I not only thought I probably couldn't do it, but it didn't sound like something Sue or I would really want to do.

Arnold is a good friend and a very kind person and he really wanted to help me. He knew my daughter, Krissy, had recently married and her husband was out of work. He suggested since I didn't want to do it, my daughter and her husband could travel around the country selling my jewelry at his shows. He promised me he would personally look after them.

That was very generous of him and it was a great idea. At Arnold's suggestion, two spaces that were next to each other with tables and showcases were provided for us at an upcoming local show in Baltimore. Sue and I would work behind one booth and my daughter and her husband behind the other. This would enable me to teach and supervise them. I would only have to make it through this one weekend. I thought I could pay them well giving her husband a job and I believed it would be rather easy and fun for both of them. There really wasn't much training required as all of the jewelry we had was purchased from closed jewelry stores and every single piece had a tag with the jeweler's retail price. I told Krissy to simply take 80 percent off of that retail price which would still give us a good profit.

She didn't have to know much about jewelry because most of the buyers were jewelers and our price was usually far below their wholesale cost. It was a perfect set up for her and her husband and would solve a big problem for me as well.

It was a gruesome three days. You get there early in the morning and spend about two hours setting up. Then you spend about eight hours standing on your feet on a cement floor waiting on customers. After the show closes, it takes about an hour to close down and put all the jewelry into the show's lock up. It's a long hard day and my deadbeat, 22-year-old, healthy son-in-law, hated it and said the work was just too hard for him, even though I paid him more for those three days than he made in a month at his last job working at a Seven-11.

Surprisingly, in spite of the long days and hard work, Sue and I really had a great time. We met so many interesting people and had a lot of fun. Most important of all, we liquidated more inventory in those three days than I would have imagined was possible.

At the end of the show, Arnold asked me how my daughter and her husband liked working the show. I told him my daughter seemed to enjoy it, but my son-in-law said it was far too hard for him and they would not be doing it again. Sue and I had a great time and were anxious to continue doing shows.

Fortunately, Krissy terminated her relationship with her husband shortly thereafter. She went on to become extremely successful in her own business.

For the next few years, Sue and I averaged about 20 shows a year. Even though it was hard work and physically draining, very often it was enjoyable traveling all over the United States and spending a couple of weekends a month in different cities. Sometimes I would complain to Sue about being tired or exhausted. She would respond by saying the hard work was good for me and constantly reminded me the shows were particularly beneficial because they provided us a means to liquidate our jewelry and reinvest the proceeds in our commercial loan business. The first year we did the shows, we didn't have much of a concern about our safety as Arnold maintained an exceptional security force at every show and we hadn't heard of anyone having any problems. We carried only enough jewelry to fill the showcases at our booth which Arnold provided.

Beginning our second year we had just arrived at the show in Santa Monica, California. We had become friends with many of the dealers that regularly did the shows. We were glad to see at the booth just to our right, Gerry, a dealer we liked very much. It was always enjoyable having our booth next to his. It was about two hours before the show was to open and the only people in the hall were employees of the promoter, dealers setting up and the security force. As usual everyone felt very safe. Gerry left his booth and placed his cases filled with his jewelry underneath his tables as many dealers were accustomed to do. A taxicab pulled up to an exit door just a few feet from us. Two men jumped out and ran directly to Gerry's booth. In seconds they grabbed his cases, ran back to the taxicab and sped away.

Gerry was devastated and told me the cases they took contained every bit of jewelry he owned. Everyone at the show was pretty shaken up. New and more stringent security procedures were put in place. Sue and I wondered if this was an isolated incident or just the beginning of a new risk we would have to evaluate before continuing with the shows.

Unfortunately, as the year progressed there were many other incidents. We learned that criminals in Colombia, South America, had been professionally trained for many different ways to rob and hold up jewelry, antique and coin show dealers. One of the favorite tricks of the criminals was to place a nail in front of the tire of a dealer with the pointed end positioned so it entered and pierced the tire as the dealer drove off, giving him a slow leak. They would do this on Sunday evening knowing the dealer will usually have his jewelry and the proceeds from his sales in his automobile. When the unsuspecting dealer, now a few miles away, stopped to change his flat tire, the criminals would pull up and volunteer to help and of course, he would be victimized. In one case an 82-year-old man, who resisted, was beaten with a tire iron.

More than once, they were successful using another clever trick. The criminals would wait at the airport for dealers from the show carrying suitcases they knew contained jewelry. As the dealer would stand in the ticket line a child carrying an ice cream cone would bump into the dealer getting ice cream all over the dealer's clothes. The child would apologize profusely as if it was an accident. The dealer would set his case down to wipe the ice cream off and while his attention was being diverted, an accomplice from behind would steal his cases and disappear into the crowd.

Sue and I had two very good friends, Bob and June, we associated with often. They were a married couple living not far from us in Potomac, Maryland. We also participated with them in several business ventures. They were fascinated hearing of our experiences traveling around the country selling jewelry at gem shows. They said they had business in Los Angeles and wanted to know if they could travel and spend time with us at our next show in California. It sounded like it would be a lot of fun and I agreed but I was concerned with Bob's cavalier attitude about the security problems I had shared with him.

At our next show in Pasadena, California, Bob and June spent the latter part of Sunday with us at the jewelry show. It was packed and everyone was very busy. I could see that Bob was really enjoying himself and several times he said how exciting he thought it all was, but he didn't see any risk or danger at all and suggested I was just being overly cautious.

Sunday night, at Los Angeles airport, the four of us waited in line behind an Asian couple who had also done the show. They were directly in front of Bob waiting to go through the security scanner. They placed their carry-on bag containing the inventory of their most expensive diamond jewelry on the scanner belt. As the couple walked through the personal scanner, a man wearing running shoes quickly ran from behind knocking Bob out of the way. He then reached into the opening where the belt was pulling the couple's bag containing their jewelry and yanked it back out. The dealer, seeing what was happening, was screaming, but was helpless as he was on the other side of the security scanner. The thief ran very fast toward a large crowd in the outer corridor and vanished with the couple's bag.

Bob was really shaken and didn't need any more convincing. He said he would never do one of these events. Sue and I felt our only substantial risk was getting the inventory to and from the shows. It was just too dangerous and both of us agreed we too would not be doing any more shows. Before we had a chance to tell Arnold of our decision, he told us he had just made arrangements for an insured armored truck service to pick up the dealer's jewelry at the closing of each show and deliver it to them at the next show.

We didn't want to stop doing the shows as we really enjoyed doing them. We had also become accustomed to scheduling our time so it didn't interfere with our lending business and we still had a lot of jewelry to sell. With these new conditions in place, we joined the overwhelming majority of dealers to use this service and decided to continue.

The armored truck service worked out really well. Robberies became extremely rare and only occurred when a dealer didn't use the armored truck service. We didn't have our jewelry with us before or after the shows and it was now nice for us to be able to stay an extra day or two to enjoy these great cities. This luxury was something we couldn't safely do before.

There were a few dealers who didn't, or couldn't, use the new armored service for one reason or another. There was a gold chain dealer that carried more than $1 million in inventory. He felt it was better and less costly for him to have his own security people with him due to the large quantity of merchandise he carried. He came and left each show in what he felt was a secure van and always had four very husky men with him. His permanent business location was only a few miles from the show, therefore he didn't have far to travel. Unfortunately his private security was not good enough. Not far from the show he was forced off the road and held up at gunpoint and lost his entire inventory.

A dealer Sue and I particularly enjoyed seeing at the shows was a man named Kenny. He carried a large line of sterling silver jewelry, some containing semi-precious stones. His inventory filled more than 20 feet of showcases. He also had one tray of men's gold and diamond rings. His silver jewelry was priced quite reasonably, but his gold and diamond rings were priced very high. I asked him why the gold rings were priced so high. He told me that he really didn't want to sell them and in all the years he did the shows, he had only sold one. He bought them one at a time and only when he thought the price was far below wholesale. He said they were his retirement plan and he only put them in his showcases because he loved having them with him and it made his display look really good.

Kenny had an incredibly good personality and always told us the best new jokes. He was always happy and was one of the most positive individuals I had ever met. Everyone loved just being around him. At a show in Chicago, we went to dinner with Kenny on a Saturday night. He was excited to tell us of a new line of silver jewelry he just acquired and had already sold over $50,000 to an Indian reservation and was going to deliver it after the show closed.

As we were leaving the show on Sunday night to head for the airport, I looked over at Kenny. He was packing up and quietly singing to himself. He looked up at me with a gentle smile and said, "Have a great trip back and don't do anything I wouldn't do." I yelled back, "That gives me a lot of latitude, doesn't it?"

The next morning I was awakened by a telephone call at about 5:00 a.m. At that time of the morning I knew it was not going to be good news. At first I didn't know who it was as the voice was trembling and inaudible. I thought it might be a wrong number. I said, "Calm down, who is this?"

The voice on the other end said, "It's me, Kenny." He said he left the show Sunday night about 8:00 p.m. He drove about 300 miles without stopping en route to the Indian reservation. He had traveled so far from the show he was certain it was safe to gas up and use the restroom. While in the restroom somebody opened the door and shouted, "If that's your large black vehicle out there you're being robbed." He said he ran out only to see a van speeding away. His vehicle had been broken into. He couldn't believe the criminals had been so patient as to follow him all the way from the show. All of his inventory including the shipment for the Indian reservation and even the gold and diamond rings were gone.

Panicked, he asked me what he could do, but I had no answers. All I could do was tell him how terribly sorry I was.

Sue and I were surprised to see Kenny at the next show. He had re-stocked with merchandise on consignment and told us the criminals may have gotten his entire inventory, but he wasn't going to let them ruin his life. He would just have to start over.

Even though it was terrible for Kenny and the gold chain dealer, al-most every other dealer used the armored service so robberies were very rare. Usually there were between 200 and 500 dealers at a show. In those days there were dealers on a waiting list to get into the shows. As soon as a dealer discontinued doing the shows, a new dealer took their place. Most were genuinely nice people and I respected them for the long hard hours they worked. We acquired many new friends and probably the most enjoy-able thing about doing the shows was having dinner and socializing with them in the evenings after the show closed.

After a couple years of doing the shows we were introduced to Harry and Jane, a new dealer and his wife. They told us they had always worked and did everything together, just like Sue and I; and like us, he too had pur-chased large inventories of jewelry during the bad economic recession. They dressed exceptionally well, were very fit and attractive and had a very professional appearance. I believe they were both in their late 30s or early 40s. Jane was particularly quiet and demure and always looked prim and proper. She used no makeup and wore only dresses with high collars, never a plunging neckline. Harry boasted of Jane's dedication to her exceptional baking abilities and about the National Betty Crocker Bake Off Contest she had won. He sparkled with pride as he described in detail the bright blue ribbon she received for taking first place. She would tell us how proud she was of Harry's involvement with the Boy Scouts and other nonprofit organizations. He had a private pilot's license and a black belt in karate. They were like a traditional conservative couple from the old South and, to say the least, they were very interesting.

Over the next year, we developed a very strong friendship with Harry and Jane. At the shows on Friday and Saturday evenings, we enjoyed a good dinner together. Arnold knew of the relationship we had developed with them and asked what I knew about them. I told him of what I had learned and thought they were very nice. He told me he considered them very nice, but he also thought they were a little strange. He said that one night after a show, while checking out of his hotel, Harry was standing beside him and also checking out. He said Harry was holding his briefcase and Arnold knew it contained some very expensive jewelry pieces Harry always carried with him. Arnold said he whispered to Harry that three young South Americans were sitting in the lobby just a few feet from them. Arnold told Harry he saw them at the show this weekend wandering around but not purchasing anything. It was probable that they were looking for a dealer to rob that was carrying jewelry.

The next thing Arnold told me was shocking. He said Harry turned around and stared expressionless directly at the three young men. He put his case down and with his foot he slid it across the floor directly at the three young men saying, "I dare you to touch it."

Stunned, I asked what happened next.

Arnold said the three men got up and walked out of the hotel. Harry completely unaffected picked up his case and left. I told Arnold I knew Harry had a black belt and taught classes in karate, but I had no idea he was that tough. I said I spent a lot of time with him and his wife and now would probably feel a little safer.

Curiously Harry carried a strange line of jewelry that looked more like it belonged in a high end antique shop and a variety of unusual gold and silver coins. I looked forward to seeing what new and different pieces he brought to each show. On one occasion he showed me an 18 karat men's Piaget wristwatch. I was familiar with this manufacturer and knew the original cost of this watch was about $18,000. It was used but in really good condition except for a few brown stains on its band and face. He said it wasn't in his case for display because he just acquired it in a large package of jewelry and wanted to get it cleaned before offering it for sale, but if I wanted it I could have it for only $1,000.

What an incredible bargain it was and I told Sue I thought he only let me have it for that great price because he must have purchased it very cheaply with all the other jewelry in the parcel and wanted to give me a really special deal. I sent it to the manufacturer's representative in New York. They replaced the dial and detailed the wristwatch making it look new. It fit me perfectly and I was thrilled to keep it for myself.

In early December of that year, we did a show in Seattle, Washington. We were pleased Harry and June also did the show and again went to dinner with them on Friday and Saturday night. At dinner Friday night, Harry told me he learned the South American criminals had become very active again. He said they had been trained to follow dealers back to their hotel after they left the show on Saturday. They would then know what hotel the dealer was staying at and what room he would be in. Harry said on Sunday before the show closed they would break into the dealers room and wait for him to return making him an easy target. He said because he always had to carry his most expensive pieces with him he avoided giving the criminals the opportunity to rob him because on Saturday night he would simply check out of the hotel and check into a new hotel near the airport. He suggested that I do the same as we could drive from the show Sunday night directly to the hotel and go to the airport together Monday morning. It would be safer for both of us. I said it sounded like a great idea, but I had a redeye flight leaving Sunday night and we were sending our jewelry with the armored truck service. He said that's great and he would consider that in the future.

The next night, we had dinner again and he said that he had checked the schedule and saw that the next show was in February at the Sheraton

Hotel in Lanham, Maryland. He asked me that since we had become very good friends over the past year if it would be possible for them to stay at our house in February so that we could go to the show every day together. I said sure, we have lots of room and would love to have you stay with us. We felt being together would also provide more security for all of us.

A couple of weeks after Sue and I arrived home, I received a telephone call from Harry. He told me that he had just purchased 82 gold, one ounce African Krugerrands and asked if I was interested in buying them. I said no, I wouldn't take advantage of him. I gave him the name of the person that I dealt with at Engelhard refineries that would pay him close to 100 percent of their value. He was very appreciative and said he was looking forward to seeing us in February.

About a month later, I received a call from the bureau. They said they needed to come out and talk to me. I was still working occasionally on some of their cases and assumed it must be concerning one of those but it seemed a little strange to me that the call did not come from Truman. When they arrived, they asked me what I knew about Harry and Jane. I told them everything I knew about them and about the relationship we had developed. They asked me if Harry had offered me anything recently. I told him of the call and of the 82 Krugerrands. I also told them of the Piaget wristwatch I purchased from him and asked them what was going on.

They told me Harry and Jane had been arrested in Texas. I gasped and asked, "What for?"

Then came the biggest surprise of all. Murder they said.

"Are you telling me Harry killed somebody?"

"No, he killed three people, at least that's all we know about now. We believe you and Sue were to be his next victims."

They went on to explain to me exactly what happened. Harry and his wife would attend coin, antique and jewelry shows. He and his wife would gain the trust of a dealer at the show by becoming very friendly with him. Once he was in a position to be alone with him, a male partner hiding in the shadows would kill the person and they would steal all of his merchandise. They told me about two months ago, Harry had arranged to meet one of his so-called good friends at the Orange County Airport, California. It was a dealer he met and befriended at a coin show. Harry told the dealer to bring the large quantity of gold coins including 82 Gold Krugerrands in exchange for cash. He also told the dealer not to tell anyone as he said, "You never know who you can trust," and the dealer agreed.

On the day of the meeting Harry helped his wife set up that morning at a jewelry show only a few hundred miles away. He left the show at about 10:00 a.m. and flew a private plane to Orange County Airport. After killing the unsuspecting dealer and stealing the coins, he flew back to the jewelry show and helped his wife pack up.

I understood Harry was sure to talk to many dealers at the show both in the morning and when he returned. He thought he had the perfect alibi.

I asked the agents what brought them to me. They told me that when they arrested Harry, they found written instructions of how to get from my house to Baltimore-Washington International Airport along with detailed drawings that were given to his partner.

We were told that Harry ultimately received a life sentence. The partner who actually did the killings was sentenced to death. Harry's wife Jane somehow got off scott free. We learned she never really won the Betty Crocker Bake Off contest or any other contest. We also learned the very first dealer they killed was wearing a Piaget wristwatch described exactly as the one I purchased from Harry. The bureau and I concluded the brown stains were probably dried blood.

That was the final straw for Sue and me. The next time we left town, it wasn't to attend a gem show. Most of our remaining jewelry inventory was sold by an auction company in Baltimore. Not withstanding the fact we almost lost our lives, doing the shows was great for our lending business, as every dollar we derived from the sales of the jewelry was invested into our commercial loans.

Chapter 14
Like The Blink Of An Eye

EVEN IF WE hadn't had any problems doing the gem shows it would have been very difficult for us to maintain our rigorous work schedule. Time not spent preparing for, or doing the gem shows, was consumed with our commercial lending business and a few cases we were still working for the bureau. We had very little time to ourselves, but it was difficult for us to slow down as we were accomplishing so much. We had now sold almost all of the jewelry inventory and built our commercial lending business substantially. As a matter of fact, our lending business had grown so much we needed more space and neither Sue nor I wanted to reopen an office. My health was slowly deteriorating and my doctors at Johns Hopkins advised me to exercise every day, recommending swimming because of its low impact.

We hired a crew to add a large addition to our current home and install a swimming pool. The original builder used a beautiful, but very unusual white split stone for the entire exterior of our house and we couldn't find it anywhere. We learned one of the area's largest masonry plants located in College Park, Maryland, had declared bankruptcy and its entire inventory was to be auctioned off. We attended the preview and were excited to see the exact same white split stone that was used to build our house. Incredibly, there was just enough to complete our addition.

The retail price of that stone would have been about $4000 and I would have been glad to pay it because we had not been able to find it anywhere else. Anything less than that price would have been a great savings and I guessed at the auction it probably would bring about half of the retail price. I was wrong; nobody else seemed to want it. It was one of the first items auctioned that morning and I bought it all for about $50.

There were several bundles of bricks of different varieties and enough commercial pavers to build a 2,000 square foot patio. The bricks were separated by their variety and each lot only contained between four and six cubes. Each cube contained about 500 bricks. There were very few buyers interested in purchasing or moving any of them. I couldn't help myself. I started every bid at $10 and almost all the bricks and pavers the entire day were awarded to me. By the end of the day I had only spent about $800 but had purchased what would have cost retail before the auction more than $23,000. I didn't know what I was going to do with all those bricks, but how often do you get an opportunity like this? I hardly have ever been able to turn down a bargain, and never one like this. When the auction was over, the auctioneer made an announcement we hadn't expected. He said everything had to be removed within three days; after that the bank would dispose of it at the buyer's expense.

Sue told me I had lost my mind and asked how in the world I expected to move everything I bought in such a short time. Being the good wife she is though, she spent the entire remainder of that day calling masonry movers only to be repeatedly told they could not be available to help us for at least two weeks.

I had financed a small residential homebuilder and called him for advice. He said if he were in my situation, he would get his own laborers and move the stone and bricks himself. He gave me an address in Silver Spring, Maryland where laborers wait every morning seeking work. They charged about $20 a day. I rented a large truck and Sue and I were there before 6:00 a.m. the next morning. When I pulled up about 20 men approached me, all wanting to work that day. I told them the job was moving stone and brick and would probably be the hardest work they ever did but instead of $20 I would pay $40 for the day. They all wanted to get into the truck. I chose what appeared to be the healthiest and strongest four men in the crowd.

We all worked extremely hard that day moving load after load into the backyard of my home. We only stopped for cold drinks and of course I bought everyone lunch. The way we loaded and unloaded was to have two men on the ground handing the stones to two men behind the truck who would hand them up into the truck to two others. These two would then stack the stones in the truck's bed. That took six people and our truck only had enough room for us and the four men we picked up. You guessed it; Sue and I were the other two workers. We rotated every hour so we all would be using different muscles and nobody would work any harder than anyone else. By the end of the day we had moved all of the stone, but none of the commercial pavers or bricks.

On the way back, Sue drove the truck so I could pay the men. I turned to them and said, "You men did a great job. You told me that you wanted $20 each for the day. I know I told you I would pay you $40 each, but this work was actually even harder than I thought it would be and you guys did such a great job I'm going to pay you $100 each."

They all joyfully cheered and one of the workers said, "You're the man."

"You did such a great job, we can get all of the pavers moved tomorrow and I'll pay you each $100 tomorrow as well." There was total silence. "Come on, it's $100 again tomorrow, who's on board?" Again, total silence.

After a minute or so one of the men said, "What do you think we are man, slaves?" It kind of reminded me of the gold dealer who years earlier told me he only had to work one day a week because every day he worked he made $500. The next day I had to get four new men, but I knew there was no way I could get all of the almost 30,000 bricks moved within the allotted time period.

About three o'clock in the morning I was lying awake in bed worried about what to do about all the bricks we didn't have time to move. I knew Steve, one of my borrowers, was re-surfacing a small residential house on a main road that had been re-zoned for commercial use. It was located In College Park less than a mile from the masonry plant. I only had one day left to move the remaining bricks. I couldn't wait any longer, so at three o'clock in the morning I called him. His wife answered and I told her to wake Steve, it was urgent. Steve came to the phone and asked me what was going on. I said that I noticed he was removing all the aluminum siding from his building and asked what he was going to use to resurface it.

"Are you crazy, you call me at three o'clock in the morning to ask me that? Are you drunk?"

I said I had no choice, I was on a strict deadline. I asked if he would like to have the entire building bricked at no cost to him. Wouldn't that be worth a call at this time in the morning?

"What's the catch?"

I told him I purchased far more than twice as many bricks as he would need to do his entire building and they were stored less than a mile away from him. The value of the bricks was over $16,000, but I would sell them all to him for $1,500. I told him he could use the bricks he needed and because he was on a main highway he wouldn't have any trouble selling the ones he didn't use. Even if he sold them at 80 percent off retail he would get enough money to pay for the bricks he used and the cost of installing them on his building. He would have the entire building bricked at no cost to him.

"Steve is that worth getting up at three o'clock in the morning for?"

"Sounds great, what do I have to do?"

"You have to move everything today day by 5:00 p.m."

Steve paid the $1,500 and had all the bricks moved before the deadline. After he re-surfaced the outside of the building, he had no problem selling the balance of the bricks. He actually not only got all of his money back but had made a substantial profit and said he was very grateful that I had called.

The money I received from Steve paid for my stone, commercial pavers and my cost of moving them and Sue and I enjoyed the best two days of "exercise" of our lives. Although Sue would not agree, and after more than 20 years, she still complains of the aches and pains she suffers as a result of the excruciating work she did; especially when she wants something special.

We had the addition constructed out of the white split stone and had a lovely little pool house built out of beautiful Canadian stone we purchased at the same auction. We had enough of the Canadian stone to also build a large outside fireplace and we completed the 2,000 square foot patio Sue wanted. The pool was completed about the same time and I thought maybe we could finally relax and take a short break. I could work on my health issues by exercising and swimming a little every day, something it seemed I never had time for before. However, that was not in the cards.

It wasn't long before I received the letter everyone dreads; a request from the Internal Revenue Service wanting information about my last tax return. It was the standard boilerplate form with a couple of dozen little boxes on it so the IRS could check off only the things they questioned. What concerned me most was that every single box on the form had been checked.

Shamefully, I was still using the same accountant who years earlier had caused me to pay a penalty by filing my returns a day late. He had been doing all of my accounting and tax filings for about 20 years and we had always been too busy to make a change to someone new. I should have known better, but now, because I did not take the time, I was about to pay a big price. I called him and became even more concerned when he told me many of his clients had received the same form over the years, but he had never seen every box checked before. He said this was going to be a massive audit and told me he would meet with the IRS. He didn't want me there under any circumstances. Because the audit appeared to be so extensive he would need time to find out everything they wanted. He needed to be able to discuss it with me privately so if there were any problems we would have time to come up with the appropriate answers.

I reminded him I kept extremely good records and always paid the amount of taxes I owed. I had nothing to hide or worry about and I wanted to go to the IRS office with him. I was very uncomfortable about his continued insistence that I not go with him to the audit.

I called my uncle in New York. He was a partner in one of the leading accounting firms in the city. On our family visits as a young boy, I had seen many well-known movie stars in his office. He was one of the top accountants in the country and he often testified at the request of Congress as to the potential consequences of pending tax legislation. (That was in the days when Congress actually cared about what they were signing onto.)

I told him my accountant was insisting that I not go to the audit and asked if that was good advice. My uncle asked me if I made any income I did not report or claimed any expenses that were not legitimate.

"Absolutely not." I told him I never wanted to bother him with my little tax problems as I knew all of his clients were super wealthy with very complicated tax returns.

"That's ridiculous."

He flew down and the two of us took all of my records to a meeting he arranged with the Internal Revenue Service.

The first thing the agent asked was if I made any interest income from money I had in the bank. I said, "Yes of course, probably more than $100,000." At that time the banks actually were paying about 12 percent on savings accounts. The agent handed my uncle a copy of my tax return pointing out a particular page with a space provided for the reporting of the taxpayer's interest income. In that space my accountant had typed, "None."

The IRS computers automatically compare interest banks paid to their customers with every taxpayer's return and if they don't match the computer kicks the return out for review.

Naturally it appeared to the IRS I had not reported over $100,000 of income. It was now clear why I was having such an extensive audit. My uncle asked for a few minutes to look over the return. He pointed out to the agent that although my CPA had not reported it in the appropriate place it was reported by adding it to my ordinary income on a different schedule which resulted in paying more taxes than I actually owed. Interest income was taxed at a lower rate than ordinary income. I had paid more income taxes than I owed.

When the IRS computer showed I hadn't reported such a large amount of interest income, they ordered an investigation and learned I had extensive improvements done to my home. My tax return included many deductions for repairs to real estate. They concluded the repairs were probably for my private home and were wrongfully taken as a business deduction. There were many well-known national figures at that time being charged criminally with that very violation and they assumed I had done exactly the same thing.

The agent asked if I had any work done to my home.

"Of course, lots of things; the pool, the additions, and all the other improvements."

He showed me that my return showed a considerable quantity of deductions for real estate repairs and asked, "How can I tell the real estate repairs reported were not actually work done to your personal home?"

I showed him the files of the few remaining real estate investment properties we had sold that year. They were all residential homes financed through the Veterans Administration or the Federal Housing Administration. The only work we had done to those properties were repairs that were required by those agencies to secure the financing for the buyers. My documentation and invoices matched up perfectly with the dollar amount I properly reported as a deduction. I also showed him I had paid for those required repairs with my business checks. I had the canceled checks from my personal account that were used to pay for the work done to my home. They too matched up perfectly with the invoices for that work.

I could see he was very surprised and impressed. I told him my little joke about finding a quarter and writing it down so that I could report it. He laughed and became much friendlier as he continued through the audit which was completed in just a few hours. He wouldn't say that my accountant had intentionally posted my interest income in the improper place on my tax returns in order to spark an audit, but said he had seen it done many times before in order to generate business for accounting firms. I couldn't help but wonder if that was why my accountant was so insistent about me not going to the audit.

Upon completion, the IRS agent said he had only one problem. I had written off 100 percent of the cost of my Rolls-Royce. He said because he was so impressed with my records he would allow me as much as 80 percent. My uncle said that was very fair, but I disagreed. I told the agent he had clearly learned that I report and pay taxes on every dollar I earn. I've never played tax games like some people I know using deductions such as cattle investments, where they lose money but legally write off five times the amount of their investment. They come out way ahead by paying much less overall taxes. I only bought the Rolls-Royce because it impressed my clients and actually made me money. I had paid several hundred thousand dollars every year in taxes on that money to the Internal Revenue Service. I hated that car. It was one of the worst cars I have ever owned, but it helped me acquire clients that take commercial loans from me, so I put up with it. I told him I had records documenting every time I used that car. It was for work purposes only and had less than 2,000 miles on it. I never used it for personal use. I felt so strongly I was willing to go to court over this issue.

He called in his supervisor and reviewed my return with him. Also impressed, the supervisor agreed to allow my 100 percent write off.

My audit was finished and the return remained unchanged. Even my uncle was astounded and told me he had many clients over the years that had luxury automobiles and never were any of them allowed such a deduction. This audit was far more pleasant than what I had experienced with the Internal Revenue Service a few years earlier. My uncle continued to do my taxes and I never had a tax problem again.

Arnold called and told me everything had been very quiet at the gem shows and the dealers were doing very well. He said they hadn't had any security problems since Harry had been taken out of circulation and almost all the dealers were now using the armored security service. He asked if Sue and I might want to do a few of the shows again as he knew I still had a small quantity of jewelry left to sell. I told him we had auctioned almost all of our jewelry inventory and I was having some health issues, but I agreed to do the upcoming New Carrollton show in Maryland with the few pieces I had left. It was close to my house and I missed seeing many of our old friends there.

A few days before the show opened, I was experiencing a little blood in my urine and severe pain in my urinary tract. The doctor in the urology department at Johns Hopkins Hospital took several tests and scheduled additional tests for the following week. He gave me a prescription for antibiotics and another for pain.

He thought it was probably either an infection or a kidney stone, but he wouldn't know for sure until we got all the test results.

Three days later, on a Friday, I was behind my booth at the New Carrollton show. Sue did not want to do it because of my health problem, but I insisted. My pain really wasn't that bad and I believed being busy at this show would occupy my time much better then staying at home lying in bed; there aren't many things I dislike more than that.

Cell phones were rather new back then, but I was fortunate enough to have one. About three o'clock that afternoon I received a call. The reception was very poor, but it sounded as if the caller introduced himself as being the Chief Urologist at Johns Hopkins. Immediately I wondered why the chief of the department would be calling and not my doctor. I was sure it must be very bad news.

He said he believed in being blunt. His department had diagnosed a blockage in my ureter caused by cancer and he had shown my x-rays to three different cancer experts at the hospital and all confirmed his diagnosis. My test for the following week had been canceled and I was to be there at 6:00 a.m. sharp, Monday morning for surgery to remove the cancerous ureter.

Even now I can clearly remember my first thoughts. Life had gone by so quickly, like the blink of an eye; how could it be over so soon? I had just bought a three month supply of shampoo. When they wheeled me in for surgery the surgeon told Sue he expected the cancer had spread to surrounding organs and he believed he would have to remove some of them as well.

When I awoke from surgery I was in a lot of pain. I was surprised to see the surgeon standing right there with Sue and assumed he must have very bad news. On the contrary, he told me he had used a brand-new instrument that went inside and up into my ureter. He said this small instrument did 16 different functions and explained many of them. It had a camera to see inside, a rotary tool to grind or scrape, a vacuum to suction out material, and performed a number of other tasks. He said if I had been in almost any other hospital, my ureter would have been removed. He had never seen anything like the material in my blockage and called for a cancer expert who agreed. He said they decided not to do anything except use their instrument to remove the blockage and vacuum out the material. He told me the pain I was experiencing was only from a stint he installed in the ureter to hold it open until it could heal itself; then he would have to take it out. He also took 32 biopsies.

A few days later he called and told me the biopsies showed no actual cancer, but several of the specimens showed abnormal cells had developed.

I asked him what that meant. He said abnormal cells are cells developing into cancer. I asked him how long it would take.

"There's no way of knowing, but normally it doesn't take a long time."

That was about 25 years ago.

Chapter 15
Tranquility Just Never Lasts

DURING MY CHILDHOOD and as a young adult the people I respected, including most of my teachers, assured me I had absolutely no chance of becoming successful at anything. I was always taught to respect them and I knew they were certainly a lot smarter than me, so naturally I was always very insecure. Their pessimistic attitude towards my future was always depressing, but apparently I had a burning desire to prove them wrong. I believed it was those insecurities that caused me to be active 14 to 15 hours a day ever since I can remember. I rarely slept past 4:00 a.m. and seldom retired at night before 10:00 p.m. It seems as if I have been in a never ending marathon race all of my life. Even to this day my close friends refer to me as "Mr. Faster" and are always telling me to slow down. No one has ever understood how important it was for me to succeed in achieving financial independence or of my time restraints.

By 1989 it was already six years past my 40th birthday and according to Mayo Clinic my time should have been up by now. I had far exceeded even my wildest expectations. Almost all of the jewelry had been sold and we invested everything into our commercial lending business which had become rather successful. Sue and I agreed it was time to finally start slowing down. Early that year I decided I wanted to move to the country and buy a farm. Finally, I thought I could do something I'd always wanted to do; relax, manage our business, and maybe even learn to farm a little.

Sue and I spent every weekend for more than six months doing little except looking at farms that were for sale. Even though we had done very well financially in the past several years, farms were a lot more expensive than I had anticipated.

Most people have no idea of how long it takes to accumulate a substantial cash savings. Even someone making $1 million a year, after paying about 65 percent in taxes plus normal living expenses, would find it almost impossible to save more than a couple hundred thousand dollars annually. Sue and I needed a residence relatively close to Washington and Baltimore, in order to continue managing our business. Most everything we looked at in the 200-acre range was $1 to $3 million. We soon realized that buying a large farm would be a far bigger risk than we had imagined as it would take almost every dollar of our savings and we also would have to take on some personal debt; something we had never done before. Still, we kept looking and finally located a 200-acre farm just off Interstate 70 and only 20 minutes from Baltimore and about 35 minutes from Washington. It was perfect and we were willing to take the risk. After all, business was great and so were our earnings from our lending business.

When the contract was drafted I insisted that there be no contingencies. Later Sue asked me why I had done that and I answered that I was afraid if I left myself an out, I might talk myself out of going through with it. Four days later we settled and the farm was ours. It took every dollar in our savings account and we took a loan from the Farm Credit.

Several months earlier we had planned to go to the Grand Cayman Islands for a weekend with friends. Coincidently, arrangements had been made to leave the day after we settled on the farm. The tax laws had been radically changed, limiting deductions on passive income, which caused the value of commercial properties to decline.

On the flight to the Islands, I read an article in the *Washington Post* reporting that commercial real estate prices were predicted to fall by as much as 40 percent because of the IRS rule changes and the current crisis in the savings and loan industry. At that time my business was owed about $10 million, all secured by commercial real estate. I owed the banks more than $7 million and they were holding my notes as collateral. I had just spent all of my savings, as well as gone into personal debt for the purchase of the farm. I remember the sweat pouring down the sides of my face.

That night in the hotel I laid awake wondering what would happen if all of my commercial borrowers walked away from their properties, or worse, what if the banks called in my business lines of credit. This was our first vacation in years, yet I couldn't wait to get home.

The very next morning, from my hotel room in the Grand Cayman Islands, I called my attorney, Richard Boddie, and asked what a worst case scenario would be if the bank called in my line of credit. He said some of his commercial clients were having the same concerns and I should be prepared. If the bank called in my line of credit they could give me 30 days to pay it off. If I were unable to do so, they could simply auction my notes and hold me personally responsible for the difference between the money they received from the sale of the notes and the balance I owed the bank.

I told Boddie my loans were all secured with large equities in real estate and I also had confidence in my borrowers. He said that didn't matter, if the bank is uncomfortable because my line of credit is secured by commercial loans with rapidly falling values, they may very well demand full payoff and auction the notes as they had already done to some of his other clients.

Potential bidders for the notes have no idea whether the loans are good or bad. It would be a purely speculative investment for them and his experience was that at an auction, the notes would probably bring 10 to 20 percent of their face value. For the shortfall, he said, the bank could go after everything I owned including my farm because I had signed personally as well as on behalf of my corporation to secure my line of credit.

This would wipe me out, I said. He told me that could very well happen, but I had asked him for a worst case scenario.

The reality was that even with the falling commercial market, my notes had so much equity they were still very good investments and investors far stronger financially than me were anxious to buy them. I was making a lot of money from these loans and didn't want to sell them, but the risk that the bank might call in my line was far too great. I had personally known more than a dozen millionaires who had lost their entire wealth; usually because of circumstances they never could have expected. I did not want to be one of them.

After about four nervous months, I had sold enough of the notes to completely pay off the banks and could finally breathe a sigh of relief. The income I had been making from the notes the bank had financed was now gone, but all of the interest from the remaining notes still gave me a comfortable income and I could finally get a good night's sleep.

The tranquility I was enjoying didn't last long; it never did. I not only had major health issues to contend with, but I had become burdened with two complicated and extensive legal matters in my commercial lending business. I was forced to deal with one almost immediately at the conclusion of the other. First, I learned we had been issued a bad title report on a commercial property in Alexandria, Virginia. The loan I made exceeded $1 million and was the largest loan I had given anyone up until that time. Making matters worse, I had two junior partners on this particular loan and felt responsible for their investment. The property was directly adjacent to a hospital and zoned for a senior nursing home. It was valued at over $5 million and there were several large nursing home companies wanting to buy it and willing to pay above that amount.

This was probably the most valuable property I had ever financed and I felt very secure with my investment. Every loan I made, including this one, had a title insurance policy written by a major title insurance company guaranteeing us a good and marketable title. Again, what could go wrong?

The loan was about a year old when I learned that something was wrong—very wrong. There were covenants on this property that had not been reported to us in the title examination which made the property far more difficult, if not impossible, to develop. I only had a title problem once before. The title insurance company in that case accepted full responsibility and rectified the problem immediately at their expense. This time I was not as fortunate. I reported the problem to the title insurance company; without explanation they denied the claim. The lawsuit that followed consumed most of my time over the next two years.

I hired one of the leading real estate law firms in Northern Virginia. They were the most expensive attorneys I had ever hired, but the potential losses were so great that I wanted the best. This firm had more than a couple dozen attorneys, but handling my case was one of the three main partners. He was confident of winning this case and said it would not be much of a challenge at all. My policy with the title insurance company clearly guaranteed to protect me against any unreported covenants. His confidence was reassuring and it was comforting knowing the insurance company would ultimately be held solely responsible for any losses I might incur. He said the title insurance company would most likely be ordered to pay my legal expenses as well.

The first thing the insurance company did was petition the court to assign this case to a binding arbitration commission instead of a jury in a court room. The insurance company lawyers argued aggressively for the case to be settled through arbitration, but the judge said he was not inclined to agree. Then, to my surprise and against my wishes, my lawyer told the judge it didn't matter, we could go either way. The judge said, "Okay, as long as there is no objection, I will grant the motion for binding arbitration." My lawyer could tell I was very upset and told me to calm down. We were going to win this case either way and arbitration would be much cleaner and faster.

The arbitration trial consisted of a panel of three judges and lasted more than a week. The most dramatic testimony came from the attorney that issued the title policy on behalf of the insurance company. It was revealed that he apparently knew of the damaging covenant right from the beginning, yet he intentionally withheld that information. The arbitration court found he did this because he was making a very large fee and knew no lender would fund this loan if they had any knowledge of the covenant. His actions were reprehensible. At the termination of the hearing the chief judge said she understood exactly what had happened, but they had no discretion as to the decision the court must issue. She said the law in Virginia holds that a company cannot be held responsible if their employee commits fraud. She said if this were a Maryland case the decision would most likely be completely different as Maryland does hold companies accountable even when their employee commits fraud.

It was most painful to hear her ask my attorney, "Why didn't you take this case before a jury, don't you think you would have done a lot better there?"

He timidly asked, "Can I do it now?"

"Of course not, not after a five-day trial, our decision stands. Your only option now is to litigate against the lawyer who committed the fraud."

We did sue that lawyer and easily won a huge judgment which more than would have covered any of our losses. That is of course if he had any money. After the trial he actually smirked and told us the only things he owned were the desks and furniture in his office and we could come and get them anytime.

We hired an investigating firm and they discovered he owned and operated one of the leading real estate settlement companies in the state of Virginia; closing more than 1,500 cases a month, but his only assets were his office furnishings. He had no personal assets. He was technically "judgment proof." After negotiations we settled with him for $28,000 which covered about one third of our legal fees.

Shortly before this case was over, I received a telephone call from a friend, Steve Preston, who was an attorney and practiced law in Virginia. He told me he had recently run into an old law school classmate of his at an airport. This attorney told Steve he had filed a lawsuit against his friend, referring to and naming me personally. He said it was for nonpayment of an obligation to a bank in Virginia. Steve said he told his old classmate he didn't believe it; that he must have the wrong person. Steve said, "I've known Ed for 20 years and he has the best reputation of anyone I know in the entire banking and lending industry."

Steve told me the lawyer claiming to have filed the suit responded saying, "You're wrong, he's a crook, I could just look at him and tell."

I told Steve that his old classmate was just teasing him. There couldn't possibly be any lawsuits from a bank against me; I had never borrowed a dime from a bank in Virginia. I thanked him for his concern and told him I wasn't going to worry about it and he shouldn't either. Steve though was convinced his old classmate was not making it up and called my company attorney, Boddie, relaying the conversation to him.

A couple of days later Boddie called and said he had gone to the courthouse to check out the story. It was true, a suit had been filed against me for a loss a bank incurred on one of their loans and it was for a lot of money. A borrower of theirs had left the country and abandoned a property the bank held for collateral causing them to have a loss of several hundred thousand dollars. I also had made several loans to this same borrower secured by this property and many others he owned. All of our loans were secured by first mortgages except this one, which was taken as additional collateral as a second trust behind the bank's loan.

The bank had called me years earlier and requested I assume the borrower's obligation on their loan and I had refused. I told the senior representative of the bank under no conditions would I assume this loan, but I would agree to try to market the property for them and keep his payments current. I believed there was still sufficient equity in the property to pay the bank off in full and apply a substantial amount to the loans this borrower had with me to which I would have been entitled.

After making the borrower's payments to that bank for about six months at almost $7,000 a month, the bank again called me requesting that I assume their note for several hundred thousand dollars on this property. Again, I told the representative there was no way I would accept responsibility for this loan and to just let me know if he wanted me to stop making payments.

"No, you don't have to assume the loan or any responsibility for it. Please keep making payments on behalf of the borrowers and hopefully you can get it sold."

I followed up by sending him a letter documenting our conversation. All of this happened because of the change in tax laws that caused the value of commercial properties to plummet. The original borrower had received an offer two years earlier of $2.4 million from one of the leading commercial real estate developers in the state and had turned it down. Several commercial real estate brokers assured me that they could still secure an offer of just under $1 million. Unfortunately, the brokers were wrong.

About a year later I called the bank and told them although I had kept the payments current for them, my efforts were exhausted and they could take the property. Now they were demanding that I assume the responsibility for his debt. This is what their outrageous suit was all about.

Boddie, along with his assistant, went to the office of the bank's attorney, Richard Hess, to accept my summons and pick up a copy of their complaint. As he was leaving, Hess entered the reception area and put his hand out in an effort to shake hands saying, "There's nothing personal here, we can be gentlemen about this." Hess was upset about the letter Boddie had sent to him that concluded with ... "And your statement that Mr. Primoff was a 'crook' and that you had some enigmatic ability by simply looking at Mr. Primoff to come to such a conclusion, does little to enhance your credibility." Boddie did not shake his hand and simply responded, "When I get done with you, there'll be nothing left except bleached bones." Boddie never told me about that conversation, I learned of it from his assistant.

Boddie filed a motion for the court to discharge the bank's case as they had nothing in writing holding me responsible for the obligation as the law requires. A female lawyer who worked for the law firm representing the bank told the court there were documents I signed that they would produce at trial to prove their case. She requested the lawsuit continue to give them time to do so. The judge granted their motion while adding, "You better have something in writing." I knew the only thing they had in writing was a letter from me absolutely refusing to assume any responsibility for that loan. I thought it unconscionable for them to proceed.

The state of Virginia has, what I think, is a very unusual policy of allowing a plaintiff to file a motion every single week and Fridays are put aside to hear those particular motions. For about a year they hauled me into court many Fridays with one of these ridiculous motions. Sometimes when the case was called they would simply withdraw their motion. Nevertheless, it was costing me a lot of time and expense. We suspected that was their strategy.

Finally, after about 18 months, I called the bank and told them I wanted to settle this case, but I would only meet with the CEO of the bank. Sue and I were taken into a private office at the bank and introduced to the chief executive officer and the new vice president of the bank. I was told he was the young, brother-in-law of the CEO. Before we sat down, Sue whispered to me that they were looking for my checkbook.

I asked them if they were familiar with the recent lawsuit against McDonald's. In that case a woman had spilled hot coffee on herself and asked McDonald's to pay her $300 medical bill and she was refused.

Whereupon she sued McDonald's and received a $3 million judgment against them. They too knew how ridiculous their claims were I said.

The bank had signed many false affidavits in this case and had even made false statements in their depositions as well as motions to the court. I asked if they had any idea how much trouble they could be in.

The young vice president said, "You can't prove a thing."

I told them I believed I could. I was prepared to go all the way to trial. However, I said my mother has developed Alzheimer's and recently moved into my home and is under my care. My father-in-law was just diagnosed with cancer and given only a few months to live. My plate was full, but this was to their advantage. I was willing to shake hands and pay all my attorney fees and they should pay all their attorney fees and drop the case.

"If you agree, we'll all walk out of here and you and I will never have to see each other's ugly face again."

The young, arrogant vice president laughed and asked, "And what if we say no, what are you going to do?"

"You don't want to know, don't be so smug. Next year you may be working for me."

The CEO didn't laugh at all. He actually stood up and politely shook my hand and asked me to give them until the end of the year to think about it.

"No, it's the 15th of December and what I'm offering you is a Christmas gift. If it's not accepted by the 25th of December, I withdraw my offer."

I did not hear from them and on December 26 the bank was served with my lawsuit against them for $10 million. They no longer retained Hess as the chief counsel for this case. They immediately hired a new attorney who was a senior partner of a "silk stocking," powerhouse law firm in from New York City. Up until now the bank had refused to give my attorney access to the bank's records, but with the trial date nearing, Boddie convinced the judge to issue an order requiring the bank to immediately release all of their records.

Boddie told me to meet him at the bank at 10:00 a.m. Friday, to review all of the bank's files. When Sue and I arrived for the scheduled meeting I was furious when we were told it had been canceled and to go home.

An hour later we were in Rockville, Maryland, about halfway home when Boddie called and asked why I wasn't at the bank. I told him what happened and asked why he wasn't there. He said when he got there earlier, they were still refusing to show us the files. He left, drove directly to the courthouse and visited the judge in his chambers. The judge called the bank officers telling them if we didn't get to see the records that day, somebody at the bank would be spending the night in jail. Boddie told me to head directly back to the bank.

When we arrived at the bank there was chaos everywhere. We were taken into a room and files were being brought to us from several different employees. In the room with us was a young female lawyer representing the bank I had not seen before. Boddie asked her to leave the room and she refused. He picked up the telephone on the conference table and called the same judge who had ordered the bank to give us access to the records. Boddie told him he was on a speakerphone and the bank's lawyer refused to leave the room. The judge asked the young lady how long she had been a lawyer. "Just a few months your Honor."

"Would you still like to be a lawyer in a few months from now? If you don't leave immediately you won't be. Didn't they teach you attorney client privilege at the law school you attended?"

"Of course your Honor, but what if they steal some of the records?"

He told her to get a chair and sit outside the room and watch us through the window.

By now it was about 2:00 p.m. and the bank closed in only two hours. There was no way we were going to get through all the hundreds of files. I believed this was my last chance to prove my case and I was very worried. Who would possibly believe me over several bank officials? Could anyone on a jury possibly imagine officers of a respected bank withholding documents and fabricating falsehoods against a small private person? How unfair I thought it would be if this bank's manufactured charges against me would be a nail in my coffin.

Boddie started at the top searching through file after file looking for anything that could help. I noticed at the very bottom of one of the stacks was a file folder of a completely different color than all the rest. I pulled it out, opened it and couldn't believe my eyes. There were the minutes of the board of directors meetings the bank had claimed did not exist. The minutes revealed there were discussions between the directors trying to get me to assume the loan and of my refusal. There was even a copy of a government audit by Resolution Trust that revealed they had asked the bank if they had tried to get me to assume the loan and there it was, the bank's own written response, the "smoking gun." They had tried and tried but they said I would not assume any responsibility for the obligation. Also in that file was the letter I had written more than a year ago refusing to assume or accept any responsibility for the loan. Yet an officer of the bank had signed an affidavit stating, "No such letter ever existed."

We didn't have access to a copy machine, but I did bring my tape recorder and Boddie read into it every document from that file. The lady attorney saw what we were doing and tried frantically to open the locked door. As we left she demanded my tape recorder. Of course we ignored her.

The bank's lawyers filed an emergency motion for the court to forbid us from using any of the information that was in that particular folder. He argued the bank had given us that folder in error and cited banking regulations that protected those documents as private correspondence between the bank and the United States Government. The law did not permit them to be available to anyone else under any circumstances. The judge said he was aware of the law protecting those documents and agreed we should not have seen them. Yet, he pointed out that we didn't steal them, the bank had voluntarily showed them to us. Therefore, they were no longer protected and he would allow them to be used in the trial.

Bank officials had lied in open court and signed false affidavits. They knew they were in trouble. The very next morning I received a call from Boddie. He said we were on a conference call with the bank's attorney in New York and they wanted to accept my offer.

"What offer is that?"

"The one you made where they pay their attorney fees and you pay yours and we end this case now."

"You must be kidding, that deal was a Christmas gift they refused and we are long past that deadline."

Their attorney asked, "Will you settle if the bank pays all their attorney fees and also pays all of yours?"

"What about the pain the bank caused me and my wife over the past two years with their totally fabricated charges?"

"What if the bank pays all the attorney fees on both sides and gives you $15,000?"

"Do you think you are talking to the homeless? Add a couple of zeros to your offer and call me back."

Then Boddie spoke up, "Don't hang up Ed, be reasonable, they want to settle this now. What will it take?" I asked Sue what she thought and she said, "I won't be happy until I see the CEO of that bank running from the '60 Minutes' cameras with a raincoat over his head."

The bank's new lawyer from New York was actually a really decent and quite nice person. He met with us over lunch to personally hand us the bank's settlement check. My lawyer later told me that after we agreed to settle he learned that the CEO of the bank was listening on the conference call and when he heard Sue make the remark about him running with a raincoat over his head, he told his lawyer to give them whatever it takes. We signed a confidentiality agreement not to disclose the amount of the settlement. However, the bank was sold soon after and I believe the amount of the settlement forced an unwanted transfer of ownership.

These two lawsuits totally consumed about three years of our lives. Maybe now, I could finally settle down and do a little farming.

Chapter 16
Who Really Won The Lottery Of Life?

IT WAS THE mid-1990s and Bill Clinton was president. It made my blood boil when I heard him say that business people should pay more taxes because, "They won the lottery of life." Unless winning the "lottery of life" means working 12 to 15 hours a day often with unwavering pressures and no assurances of success. Those are the conditions the successful business people I know live with regularly. I can say with certainty, I never met anyone successful in business that worked only eight hours a day. I believe I'm more than qualified to draw that conclusion as I've financed and been intricately involved with more than 1,000 businesses of all different types; not to mention what I've experienced in my own companies.

President Clinton's remarks were so demoralizing and discouraging, they personally made me not want to spend any more time at the same rapid pace I had been working all of my life; especially now with whatever few years I had left. I felt I had earned the right to slow down and just do a little farming.

Well, at least my worries about the bank calling in my line of credit, the IRS audits, and the two major lawsuits were all behind me. My net worth now reached just into the eight figures and I had an excellent income from my commercial lending business. I was now more than 10 years past the predictions of the Mayo Clinic doctors and couldn't help wondering how much longer I could possibly have left.

My doctors at Johns Hopkins Hospital expressed concern about my current test showing I had recently developed serious lesions on both of my kidneys and my abdomen was slowly deteriorating, just as the Mayo Clinic had predicted. Sue had become extremely competent in managing our commercial loans without much help from me. For now, I was going to take time to learn how to grow some vegetables.

I bought a used commercial tractor and all the accessories including a two row corn planter. I had no idea what I was doing, but I plowed and disked about a half dozen acres until the ground looked ready for planting. With the corn planter I seeded and fertilized the six acres of ground I had just prepared and the rest of the land I rented to a local farmer. The corn came up and so did the weeds. In fact, I quickly learned that weeds grow much faster than corn. I found myself in the corn field every day for several hours trying to keep the weeds from overtaking the corn. My crop turned out okay but I couldn't understand after spending countless hours pulling weeds, how there were still more weeds than corn. I didn't understand. Once, I even noticed a farmer had pulled his tractor to the side of the road to watch me pulling the weeds away from the cornstalks and laughing as he drove away. How do the farmers do it? There were thousands of acres of corn being grown throughout the county; they didn't have weeds. There must be a trick to it.

Since moving into this county I had been too busy to socialize or meet any of my farming neighbors, but I needed to know their secret. I walked across the street and introduced myself to Eddie Rash. He was so incredibly friendly and he too laughed when he told me how he watched me everyday pulling the weeds in my corn field. He said there is no trick to it; you just have to use a chemical called Atrix. That keeps everything from growing except the corn, but I couldn't buy it because only professional farmers with a chemical applicators license could purchase it. He said many farmers pay someone else with this license to spray their fields. If I was only doing half a dozen acres he didn't think it would be easy for me to hire somebody that would agree to spray such a small area. I asked if I could get this license myself.

"You don't want to do that, you'd have to take classes and pass exams."

That afternoon Sue and I drove to the agricultural extension service and signed up for the next available classes. Later that year I was using Atrix and I never had a weed problem again. The chemical license came in rather handy as I had also planted more than 100 fruit trees that needed regular chemical spraying.

One summer night, about 8:00 p.m., I was laying on the ground hammering against the shaft on my bush hog. I had no problem putting it on, but I could not get it to release from my tractor. Harold Mercer, a neighbor I didn't know very well drove by and saw me banging on the back of the tractor. He turned his truck around and pulled behind my tractor and asked me what in the world I was doing. I told him I couldn't get the shaft to release. As he shook his head in amazement he told me that banging on it wasn't the answer, it simply needed a little twist and turn. He took it right off with ease and held it up showing me how I had bent it out of shape almost destroying it. Then he then took my hammer and spent about 30 minutes pounding it back into usable condition. It was now about 8:30 p.m. and I asked him what time he started that morning. He told me he farmed thousands of acres throughout the county and always starts his day at about 4:00 a.m.

I was rather touched. He had been working 16 hours and certainly was very tired when he stopped to help me; someone he hardly knew. I soon learned farmers were among the hardest working people and of the highest character of anyone I had ever known. I met so many wonderful people when I joined the Farm Bureau and was pleased and privileged to have them as new friends. My uncertainty about whether I made the right decision moving to this farming community were now gone. I had made a great decision.

Through the county agricultural extension service Sue and I successfully completed all of the classes and other requirements to become officially certified as Master Gardeners. My old friends from the city were visiting my farm regularly and leaving with trunk loads full of the largest, sweetest corn they had ever seen or tasted, as well as a variety of tomatoes, peppers and other vegetables. We had such an abundance, that a friend of ours who was a college professor at the University of Maryland arranged for large quantities to be given to local shelters. I also grew some of the best apples, pears, plums and peaches.

I loved this lifestyle and the new friends we made in this farming community, but my income was diminishing rapidly. Many of our older loans were paying off and we hadn't been replacing them.

The hardships we experienced with the two previous lawsuits and President Clinton's unfriendly attitude towards successful business people had discouraged me from issuing any new loans. It had been more than a year since we accepted or approved even one new loan. I knew if we didn't get back to work eventually all of our loans would be paid off and we would be forced to live solely from our savings.

Farming was great, but there was certainly no money in it, at least not for me. I heard a story about three men who were asked what they would do if they won the lottery. The first was a lawyer. He said he thought real estate was a great investment and that's where he would put his money. The second was a doctor and he said stocks were the place where he would invest. The third was a farmer. When asked, he said, "If I won the lottery, I would just keep on farming until all the money was gone."

It was a funny story, but I wondered how much truth there was in those lines. I knew so many real stories of business people who had so easily lost everything and I understood clearly it could happen to anyone. I couldn't continue farming and living only off my savings. Sue had worked harder than any woman I had ever known and she supported me faithfully in every one of my crazy endeavors. I wanted to be assured she would at least be comfortable and secure when my time was up. I also had a daughter to worry about. It was not a difficult decision to make. Like it or not, I had to go back to work.

Commercial real estate prices had stopped falling and were actually turning around and rising once again. Some of the banks I dealt with in the past were soliciting me to reopen my lines of credit. I think because of the mental relaxation and good physical exercise I got working on the farm, my health seemed to have gotten a lot better. I wasn't having many health issues at all and I hadn't felt this good in over 25 years. It was time for me to again become aggressively active in rebuilding our commercial lending business.

I reestablished several lines of bank credit and began issuing new commercial loans. I had been selective in the past with the loans I chose to fund but now I was even more demanding that the properties securing my loans have even larger equities. Our lending portfolio was increasing rapidly and I was still able to enjoy continuing my limited farming operation. Everything was going well.

One morning I was visited by Eddie Rash, my farmer friend. I could tell he was upset and I asked what was wrong. He told me the county commissioners proposed a down zoning of all the agricultural land. I asked him what that would mean to the farmers. I knew very little about agricultural zoning and nothing about the county commissioners. Frankly, I didn't even know who ran the county. I moved to Carroll County from Howard County which had an elected county executive and a council that headed up the government. Carroll County on the other hand was completely different. Three elected commissioners ran the entire show. Together, they made all the primary decisions.

Eddie told me his family had worked his farm for three generations. He, his two brothers and sister were now the sole owners. Before zoning regulations were enacted in the 1960s they could develop their entire 450-acre tract in any manner they desired. He told me neither he nor any of the other farmers opposed the zoning regulations put in place in the mid-1960's restricting property owners to one building lot for each acre they owned, rather many supported it. Nor did they oppose the more restrictive regulations enacted in the late 1970s further reducing their development rights to only one building lot for every 20 acres they owned. Now, the new county commissioners wanted to allow them only one building lot per 100 acres. That would apply to all agriculturally zoned property. Eddie told me he was getting up in age and was concerned the new restrictions, if enacted, would greatly diminish the value of his family farm.

The only retirement plan he and most of the other farmers had was the value of their land. Reducing their development rights also posed another very real problem. Farmers in the county use their property as collateral to secure bank loans every spring to pay for their farming operation. When they harvest in the fall, they pay their loans off. He told me many farmers throughout the county were very concerned that if their property was diminished in value they may not have enough equity to borrow the money they needed to cover their farming expenses.

I told Eddie he should call the county commissioners and explain what the result of the down zoning would mean to the farmers and I'm sure they would be more than willing to reconsider their position. He told me he and several other farmers had already called the commissioner's office, but they refused to meet with them. Eddie said there was one particular commissioner who really was in charge and controlled the commission. His name was Ben Brown. I told Eddie that I was accustomed to working with business people regularly and was sure I would have no problem arranging a meeting with Commissioner Brown.

I naively believed when I explained the problem to the commissioners, they would be more than willing to meet with the farmers and arrange some sort of agreeable compromise. It was inconceivable to me the county commissioners would enact legislation that would damage the farmer's ability to continue their operations. I made several calls to Commissioner Brown, but every time I was told he was unavailable. I was faithfully promised he would return my call, but he never did.

After a couple weeks, I visited the Westminster offices of the Commissioners. When I asked to see Commissioner Brown, the receptionist told me he was busy and wasn't seeing anyone. I had never met Brown but I had a description of him and I could clearly see him sitting in his office reading a newspaper. I walked past the receptionist directly into his office and told him I only needed a couple of minutes of his time. His immediate response was to tell me to get out of his office or he would call the Sheriff and have me thrown out of the building.

"I will leave, but first I'll just say one thing. I've heard of your arrogance towards the very people you are supposed to represent; now that I've seen it for myself I'll make you one promise. You have less than two years left in your position, enjoy it. I will spend the next two years ensuring that when I'm done you won't be able to win an election for dog catcher in this county."

He had no idea of my tenacity. He smiled and said, "Get out."

I was furious and in the habit of keeping my promises. I called Eddie and told him he needed to come to my house that night and bring with him five of the leading farmers in the county. When they arrived they expressed their concerns about Brown's agenda of cumbersome new regulations making it very difficult, if not impossible, to continue their farming operations. Especially, in light of his new proposal to down zone their properties. I told them of my experience with Brown and that I understood their frustration. I said this is a farming community and you don't realize how much power you have. You don't have to put up with an arrogant pompous Commissioner like Mr. Brown. I told them I was willing to help and give it all I had but they also had to make a commitment to do the same. I said we can build the largest and strongest citizens group in the county. We could throw Brown out and elect three new, decent, reasonable commissioners.

They asked what they would have to do. I explained I didn't know very many people in the county and I would have to count on each one of them to bring at least six farmers to the next meeting. I said we would have regular meetings. They asked if we'd have these meetings every month. I said no, for the time being we will meet every week. Everyone committed that night and the following week there were almost 40 people at my house.

We named our group the Carroll County Landowners Association and within a couple of months the group had grown to several hundred people. A very liberal editor of one of our County newspapers I'll call, Mr. Stu Pididiot, supported Ben Brown and his anti-property rights positions. He seemed to enjoy writing editorials making fun of our organization and downplaying any influence we could possibly have in the upcoming election. The almost daily criticism from the press caused many organizations throughout the county to become curious about our Landowners Association and often asked me to be their guest speaker. As such, I would explain what the county was doing to these farmers. I would show them articles that were provided to me by some of the older members of our group dating as far back as the 1950s. The county commissioners had placed advertisements in *The Baltimore Sun* newspaper encouraging people to come to Carroll and pursue a farming career. They were promised if they worked hard and their farms were successful, one day they would be able to retire owning a valuable piece of land. Eventually residential development would move from Baltimore and Washington to the suburbs and they would have made a great investment. I explained how the new burdensome regulations would make it difficult for the farmers to make any profits on their farming operations. I told of many farmers throughout the county who had worked full-time jobs for more than 40 years coming home everyday only to change clothes and work their farms into the night. Most often, they farmed all day Saturday and Sunday too. I would mention some of the popular farmers that many people at these meetings knew and told them what they didn't know was that many of these farmers had raised their children without ever having time to take them on a vacation.

Now, as predicted, residential development had moved into this county. Most people were outraged to hear of the county commissioners plans to take the development rights away from the farmers just to make their farms aesthetic easements for the new residents to enjoy.

So many non-farmers were joining our group, we were forced to change our name from the Carroll County Landowners Association to the Carroll County Landowners and Homeowners Association. By the end of our first year we had enrolled more than 2,300 families and were forced to hold our meetings in larger and larger facilities.

Realizing our possible political influence, editor Stu became extremely aggressive, criticizing our organization and publishing ridiculous editorials and letters to the editor from our opponents who falsely wrote of our property rights objectives. For example, on one occasion the newspaper printed, "The Landowners Association doesn't believe in any zoning laws at all; if they had their way they would put a gas station on a residential property between two residential homes." The newspaper published many of these ugly articles and letters to the editor implying the farmers didn't care about the land and were concerned only about how much money they could make.

The truth though was that nobody loved or took better care of their land than the farmers. They had sacrificed so much and worked so hard, it hurt me deeply to read such ugly, outlandish false statements. Other than voting I had never been involved in any way with politics, but this experience caused me to become more determined than ever to see that, in the upcoming election, the commissioners would be replaced by decent, honest candidates who would treat the farmers and property owners fairly.

The Carroll County Landowners and Homeowners Association was growing so fast we were mentioned in the local newspaper almost on a daily basis and always in a negative light. Some employees in the county office building began informing me of all sorts of improprieties taking place in our county government. The corruption and sex scandals of high level people in the administration seemed overwhelming and the more I learned of it, the more I became obsessed with trying to clean it up.

It was now less than a year until the election and usually everyday all of my time was spent with something involving advancing the association's objectives. Both Sue and I attended county meetings on many days and sometimes long into the evening. We believed it was absolutely necessary for us to participate in numerous county sponsored focus groups which were nothing more than a smokescreen to make it appear as if the county commissioners had included the citizens in the land planning zoning decisions. Although we knew the county would ignore the recommendations of these groups, nevertheless, the local press attended these meetings so we felt it was important for us to be there to represent the landowner's positions. There were few days our time was not consumed with county issues and we still had a business to manage.

I was becoming very tired, in fact, exhausted. I began developing some very undesirable health problems once again. It was getting very hard for me to breathe. Eating even the smallest of meals would cause my stomach to become extremely enlarged causing excruciating pain. I let no one in Carroll County know of my situation.

Dr. Hendrix at Johns Hopkins told me my abdomen was almost completely decomposed. The damage had become so extensive artificial fabric repair methods would not be possible. He had always told me there was a possibility this could happen, but also said if it did there was no known repair. He said that my condition had now become so acute that even though there was no known remedy something had to be done soon or I would not survive much longer.

Dr. Paul Manson was a top reconstructive surgeon at Johns Hopkins Hospital. He and Dr. Hendrix came up with a plan to build me an entirely new abdomen. They would take fascia off the surface of the muscles in my right leg and cut them into very small string like strips. They would use these strips to literally weave an entirely new abdomen between my stomach and my outer skin. The operation would take more than 11 hours and there was no guarantee I would survive this long procedure. Dr. Manson and two other Johns Hopkins surgeons would simultaneously perform the operation. They explained it had never been done before and the risk was enormous. I believed I really didn't have any choice; there were still many unfinished objectives I needed to complete.

Obviously I survived the operation. When I awoke my waist had been pulled from over 40 inches to less than 32 inches. I looked great and was experiencing only the normal pain one would expect after such surgery. I was breathing better than I had in years. The doctors told me I wouldn't be able to walk for about a week and with therapy I could probably be released from the hospital in about another week. I told them I was the spokesman for an association in my county and I had to attend an extremely important scheduled hearing in four days. They said the only way they could release me was if I could walk completely to the end of the hall and back by myself. They didn't think I would be able to do that without extensive physical therapy in less than two weeks.

At that time I couldn't even stand up by myself, but by that evening with Sue holding me up on one side and a nurse on the other, I was walking. I forced myself to ignore the pain and walked several times everyday. In four days I surprised my doctors by meeting their requirements and they agreed to release me. However, I still had drainage tubes on both sides of my body emptying into bottles connected to my waistline. Still the doctors allowed me to be discharged as they knew how important it was to me. When I left Johns Hopkins Hospital, Sue drove me directly to the scheduled hearing where I testified on behalf of the association with drainage bottles taped on my right and left side.

The successful operation gave me new energy and I aggressively pursued building the association's effectiveness toward the upcoming election. Every week, we were flooded with applications for new membership which increased the enthusiasm of all the current members. Now some very high-level county employees were surreptitiously supporting us as well as some unexpected important business leaders who were surprisingly rather open about it.

A few months before the election, I received an unsolicited telephone call from a powerful member of the planning commission; someone I hadn't had the opportunity to associate with before. He was anxious to meet over breakfast to discuss something he said was of the utmost importance. I met him at a local restaurant the very next morning. After the usual niceties, he said he wanted to explain how valuable my 200-acre property could be.

I told him it was as valuable as it needed to be and explained my property was zoned differently than most farms. About half was zoned agricultural, the other half conservation. I did not have any ambition to alter the development requirements in the conservation zone where almost all of my development rights were derived. I could subdivide 41 residential building sites on my property and that was more than I ultimately would intend to do anyway. The proposed agricultural change would have had little effect if any on my farm.

He went on to say that my property was in the southern end of the county, closest to Baltimore and Washington. This is where most of the development in the county was occurring. He said there was a strong possibility that my farm could be rezoned to R40, giving me about 200 development rights and that could make me a rich man. I asked him what he wanted.

"Let me be frank, Mr. Brown is impressed with you and wants you in his camp."

"Is that what this is all about?"

We had ordered breakfast but it hadn't arrived. I stood up and said, "I am already as rich as I want to be."

I threw a $20 bill on the table and told him I lost my appetite, but I'd pay for breakfast. I asked him to please do me one favor. Tell Mr. Brown that he has hurt a lot of good people and I intend to keep my promise to him.

The Carroll County Landowners and Homeowners Association held the county's most predominant forums and invited all of the candidates,

Republicans, Democrats and Independents, to speak. We booked the largest venues we could find in the county but still there was standing room only with overflow into the halls. Shortly before the election our association had several meetings to choose what candidates we would recommend. Most of the people who were running I still didn't know very well, so I had little to do with the decision. The choices were made by the overwhelming majority of the longtime residents of the county who were members of our association.

We sent out tens of thousands of letters recommending three specific Republican candidates; Donald Dell, Robin Bartlett Frazier and Julia Walsh Gouge. Editor Stu wrote scathing editorials against Dell and Frazier and explained in detail why they had little or no chance of winning the election.

On Election Day a sitting commissioner's wife approached Sue and I and angrily told us she did not appreciate our participation against her husband. She literally screamed at us, "You're messing with our business."

As I stated before, I had never been involved in politics before and was really taken back by her statement. I wondered how many other politicians view their elected positions as their business rather than public service.

When the results were finalized, all three of our candidates had handily won the election. Brown lost his bid for office by a very large margin and never won another election again.

Chapter 17
Standing Firm

NATURALLY, EVERYONE IN the association was excited with the results of the 1998 election. Donald Dell was a long time resident and farmer of the county and a person I had come to know as someone of the highest moral character. Robin Bartlett Frazier was a young mother and devoted wife who had a commercial banking background. Editor Stu's constant criticism of her during the campaign always centered on one thing, she was just too religious, claiming that would affect her ability to govern. For me, it was her most important asset.

I didn't know Julia Walsh Gouge very well, but I was familiar with a businessman, Harvey Tegeler, an honest, strong conservative, who would have been my choice. Gouge was chosen because she was one of Eddie Rash's closest friends and had promised him, his two brothers and sister, that if elected she would help them fulfill their lifelong dream of developing their farm into an 18-hole golf course subdivision. This along with the fact that she presented herself to be a strong property rights advocate made her the choice of the group.

As a guest speaker at one of our association meetings she told the group that the Rash properties location made it perfectly suited for a golf course community. It was in the southern section of the county in which almost all development was occurring.

"No other site in the county would be more appropriate," she said.

Gouge also told us her father was a farmer all of his life and upon his retirement, sold his farm for residential development. She claimed to understand the plight of the farmers and told us she was a strong property rights advocate.

About a week after the election I was surprised when Gouge called me and asked if I would have lunch with her. Sue and I met her at Rudy's Restaurant in Carroll County. She was very curt and asked me what I wanted. I asked her what she meant.

"Come on, you and your association didn't support me for nothing. Surely, you want something."

Sue and I were shocked. I told her I founded the association only because of the high level of corruption in the county and I expected her and the other two commissioners to finally clean up the county government.

"All we want is for the commissioners to be fair and honest, nothing more." We left that lunch feeling very uneasy about this commissioner, but hoped our concerns were unfounded.

I couldn't help but wonder how much more I could have accomplished if I had put as much effort into my business as I had in my political involvement in Carroll County. At least now I was secure in the knowledge that I could devote all of my time and attention to our commercial lending business.

The banks had confidence in us and we loved the lending business. I had no trouble establishing lines of credit with several new banks as well as keeping the ones I had previously established. It was as if I had no borrowing limit; $10, $20 or even $30 million in business loans was not a problem for us.

I initiated a program to acquire new and better loans. We began funding a much larger variety of businesses than we had ever done before. Soon we were getting requests from every kind of business you can imagine and we were issuing great loans; as always, secured with real estate.

We were now doing business in several different states and operated as far away as Texas and California. Many of our borrowers became great friends. One of them headed up a national company that you would know well. He was often on television as one of the top real estate tycoons teaching others how to make money in real estate. He was a fun person to

be with and I always enjoyed his company. I financed most of his purchases, especially early in his career.

I had one primary rule in approving a loan; there must be so much
equity in the real estate that I would have little concern whether the borrower repaid. My investment would be secured based solely on the equity in
the real estate. It was rare for me to ignore this requirement.

One day I received a request from a young couple, Mr. and Mrs.
Morton. Two years earlier they purchased an established restaurant business
and all of its contents. The purchase did not include the building, but the
seller agreed to rent it to them for two years. The agreement stated at the
termination of the two years, if all of the rental payments were made on
time, the seller would sell the Morton's the real estate for $400,000. When
they purchased the restaurant it was doing an annual business of about
$300,000 a year in gross sales. The couple and their children worked long
hours with determination night and day for almost two years and increased
its volume to over $1.5 million a year; a remarkable accomplishment. I was
impressed and wanted to help them.

They were such a lovely young couple and had worked so hard, but
the building was barely worth what they were paying. Issuing this loan
would break our most fundamental rule; there would be little if any equity
in the property. I felt I had no choice; I had to turn down the request.

The following day, I received a call from the broker who originally
made the request on their behalf and said he wanted to tell me an interesting, but sad story. He told me he knew the Morton's well and had been
involved with them from the beginning. The person the Morton's
purchased the restaurant from was a wealthy entrepreneur whose name I
recognized instantly. He originally purchased the restaurant for his much
younger wife who was about half his age. She was unsuccessful at running
the restaurant and was losing money every month. To purchase the
restaurant the Morton's gave the seller $250,000, which was their entire
savings.

The Morton's believed if they completely remodeled the restaurant
and worked hard they could turn it around and make it a great success.
They assumed at the end of two years they would have no problem acquiring a bank loan to purchase the building. Everything worked out great,

except they couldn't get a bank loan even though they agreed to use their private home with its small amount of equity, as additional collateral.

The seller had no obligation to extend the lease and the original contract clearly stated that if the Morton's didn't buy the building by the end of the two-year lease they would lose the restaurant, its contents and all of their original purchase money. The broker told me the seller was certain the Morton's could not get the purchase money to buy the real estate and in his words, "chomping at the bit" to get the restaurant back.

I told the broker to schedule the settlement and a few days later the Morton's owned the building. They always paid their mortgage payments before the due date. In less than two years, they secured a low interest bank loan paying off their obligation to me. I've been told the restaurant became the most successful restaurant in Baltimore and often when I pass it, I see crowds of people outside waiting to be seated. I have always enjoyed making money, but it is experiences like this that make our business wonderful.

On another occasion I received a request for a loan on a shopping center in College Park. The person that owned the shopping center died and had told his wife to sell it only to his best friend, Mr. Cassidy, who had a small restaurant within the same center. He had also instructed his wife to sell it for $750,000 even though the center was worth more than twice that amount.

The attorney that referred this loan to me said that Cassidy had $350,000, but needed to borrow the balance. He did not meet the bank's income requirements. He said I was his last hope or the property would be sold on the open market. It was a great loan and we approved it without hesitation.

Cassidy told me the dry cleaner at the corner of his center had been paying the same $800 a month for the last 20 years. He offered them the opportunity to remain at a slightly higher rental rate, but they chose to relocate. Subsequently, he rented their space to a national fast food chain for $3,600 a month. The other tenants who would not agree to an increase left and Cassidy also received much higher rent from those spaces.

Later he told me he was making more money off the rental income than he ever made in his small restaurant. The last time I talked to him he was purchasing another piece of commercial property.

I had some close friends who wanted to participate in my lending business. They had capital to invest and the return on the money I was lending was a far better return than they were receiving elsewhere. Plus, the risk was much smaller. A few years back I had agreed to take on a couple of partners on a few of my loans and I had a very bad experience with both of them. I did all the work, they did all the complaining. Therefore, this time, I was even more selective with whom I would agree to participate in my business investments.

A good friend, who was a very successful retired attorney, told me his accountant was seeking a lender for one of his clients. He asked if I would check out the loan request. If it was a good loan, he wanted to do it with me. The company requesting the loan was being pressured to join a local union and desperately needed the money to continue their battle to resist. He said the loan request would obligate us for about $1.5 million. It would be secured by one of the largest laundry companies in Washington and with their real estate valued at more than $5 million.

You can only imagine my surprise when he told me the name of the company. It was the very company that employed me as a laundry route man 38 years earlier. Yes, the same company that refused to let me leave early in the day even though I had built the revenues of my route higher than anyone else in the company.

I did not tell my friend of my past relationship with this company until after we evaluated the property and both had agreed to do the loan. He asked why I didn't tell that story to the owner of the company, the son of the one I had worked for, after we interviewed him for the loan. I said I wasn't there to humiliate the owner; I was there to help him and make a little money for myself.

We made the loan and everything worked out great for us and for the laundry company. That's the way it's supposed to be. Early in life I learned that I get much better results when my actions are guided to achieving the objective, rather than being influenced by my emotions. A sign in my office read:

"Here lies John Jay.
He died maintaining his right-of-way.

He knew he was right as he sped along,
But he's just as dead as if he was wrong."

Some states required lending licenses and would periodically audit the loans I issued in their state. After one such audit, officials from the state of Virginia notified me that they wanted to return to my office and discuss some of their concerns. The auditor would not discuss on the telephone why he wanted to return, but when he arrived at my home office he had only one question. How do you do so many loans in the state of Virginia and never have anyone delinquent?

I told him I never said I didn't have a delinquent borrower. Many of my borrowers pay irregularly, some not at all. The question I was asked by the state wasn't if my borrowers were delinquent. I was specifically asked how many borrowers paid satisfactory. I answered, "Every loan I have is satisfactory according to my standards." I simply have a no foreclosure policy.

He asked, "How is that possible?"

I showed him my records and pointed out that with the hundreds of commercial loans we had done, we had never foreclosed on anyone unless they had physically abandoned the property; and that only happened once or twice in his state.

"How can you possibly successfully operate in that manner?"

"Let me explain by showing you an extreme example." I opened Mr. Weston's folder to show him the history of this account. There weren't any recorded payments, but many of my handwritten notations. Several years earlier this loan was recommended to me by Mr. Laurel, a well-known and respected real estate settlement attorney. He told me Weston owned a piece of property that contained 450 acres which was zoned for one-half acre residential lots. He said Weston had a small loan on this property and was having some financial difficulties. He was in fear of losing his property and needed an immediate loan of $125,000. I asked Laurel what he thought the property was worth.

He told me he was sure it was worth more than $1 million but warned me that Mr. Weston was over 70-years-old and would probably not make many payments.

I told him with that much equity, I wasn't concerned about payments. I sent a check for $125,000 to Laurel. He prepared the paperwork and the loan settled three days later.

For five years I received no payments or correspondence of any kind from Weston, but then I received a telephone call at two o'clock in the morning. In a broken voice, Weston introduced himself and asked if I knew who he was.

"Certainly, what in the world can I do for you?"

He said and I quote, "I came down to Ocean City to hustle some women. I got drunk last night in a bar and they called the police on me. I punched a cop and I'm in jail."

"You are the only person I can turn to. You were there years ago when no one else would help me. Can you help me now? I need $1,000 for a bond."

I told him to put a policeman on the phone. The officer gave me the instructions and in the morning, Sue wired the $1,000.

Two more years went by with no payments or communication of any kind. The real estate residential development market was exploding. I received a call from Laurel who told me he had great news. Weston's property was sold and Laurel was requesting payoff figures.

I jokingly told Laurel that was not good news, that's terrible news. "That's my best loan."

That Friday, Sue answered the telephone and told me Weston was at settlement and wanted to talk to me. I expected he would be upset as the interest had accumulated with late fees for seven years and was well over the $125,000 he had originally borrowed.

I was wrong about him being upset; he was actually very emotional and told me how much he appreciated what I had done for him.

"Mr. Primoff I would have lost this property. You made me a millionaire."

I showed the Virginia auditor the settlement sheet. After paying me off along with all of his selling costs, Weston received several million dollars from the sale of his property. I also showed the auditor the Christmas cards I received from Weston the following two years after he sold his property and paid off the loan to me. I had kept them in his file.

Before the auditor left that morning, he told me he had been auditing lender's records for many years, but he had never seen any lending business run quite like this. I later received a letter from the state of Virginia. They thanked me for my participation in the audit and stated that banks and other lenders should take lessons from my business practices.

We were approaching the end of the century and things were going pretty well for me. My commercial lending business had never run so smoothly and my income had soared to figures I could have never imagined. The corrupt county commissioner had been replaced and other than receiving constant complaints from the association members about Gouge, everything else seemed to be going pretty well.

I did my best to stay out of politics, but that was not easy to do. Ellen Sauerbrey had run for Governor of Maryland and knew me through my activity with the association. She called and asked me if I would agree to be on a televised panel to oppose then incumbent Democrat Governor Parris Glendenning's "Smart Growth" agenda. Just the thought of being on television scared me to death. I did my best to get out of it, but I admire this woman so much and she is very persuasive.

Glendenning was to be on the Public Broadcasting Station show representing his position along with four Democrats and four opposing Republicans, including myself. Before the show, I corresponded with the other three Republicans. We all agreed that we would strongly oppose the governor's agenda.

At the beginning of the show, a short film was shown strongly promoting the governor's "Smart Growth" plan which included promoting more public transportation and recommending land use allowing no less than several families per acre. I think his original proposal was at least 16 families per acre. Then, one at a time, each Democrat complimented the plan. There was a lot of pressure as the public television show was, along with all the Democrats, strongly supporting the governor's plan.

I was surprised and disappointed all three Republicans caved saying they wouldn't oppose the smart growth policies, but not me. I had a 3 x 5 card on my leg with all the talking points given to me by conservative university professors who were experts in land use.

When it was my turn to speak I didn't hold back at all. I explained the terrible effects brought on by the governors so-called "Smart Growth" plan. I had a litany of problems brought on by this type of high density development. Drugs, crime and poverty are a few of the criticisms I now remember, but on the show I rattled off several more from my card.

I told Governor Glendenning, his Smart Growth program reminded me of an animal study I had recently seen on a television show. It wasn't one of the talking points given to me, but I thought it was right on the mark.

I explained that researchers had taken two mice and put them in a room and they got along very well. When they introduced the third mouse they didn't get along quite as nicely. When they added the fourth mouse there was some contention. By the time they had a dozen mice in the room, even though there was plenty of food and room for all of them, they were fighting and killing each other.

I said, "The animal rights groups call this cruelty to animals. The governor calls it, Smart Growth."

Before the show was over the phones were ringing off the hook. Every caller supported my position opposing the governor's program and he was furious.

When I arrived home that night, a well-known political conservative attorney called to congratulate me on my performance on the show and warned me to make sure that my state records were in order. I thought he was kidding, but sure enough within a few days there was a knock on my door before 8:00 a.m. It was an unscheduled audit on my lending business in the state of Maryland.

I told the auditor I couldn't believe he was auditing me as a result of my opposition to the governor's Smart Growth program.

"I don't know what you're talking about, we do unscheduled audits all the time."

I told him I had been licensed by the state for more than 20 years and had never heard of any such thing. Nevertheless, I invited him in and asked what he wanted to see.

"I want to review every one of the loans you did last year."

I said that was fine and I handed him a piece of blank paper. He turned it over and looked at the other side which was also blank and said, "There's nothing here."

I told him that was all the consumer loans I did the entire year. He told me he had checked my tax records and I had reported a substantial amount of income from my lending business on loans made in Maryland. I told him I do not make consumer loans of any kind and he had no authority to review my commercial lending transactions.

He became quite indignant and threatened to take my lending license off the wall. I took it off the wall myself and handed it to him, but he refused to take it.

I gave him my attorney's name and telephone number and insisted he leave. That afternoon he called my attorney and thankfully I never heard from him or anyone from the Department of Labor, Licensing and Regulation ever again.

That weekend, *The Baltimore Sun* printed several letters in response to the PBS show. The entire page was filled with letters from around the state supporting my anti-Smart Growth views. I stood firm in my beliefs, but I wasn't happy about becoming the number one enemy of our sitting governor. I still wondered if it was ever going to be possible for me to finally take it easy, continue a little vegetable planting, and run my lending business in peace. Being able to continue breathing would also be a nice thing.

Chapter 18
I'd Of Had To Miss The Dance

TWO YEARS EARLIER, Sue and I had become huge admirers of Ellen Sauerbrey. She was as an accomplished and talented woman as we had ever met in the political arena. She was also a strict Constitutionalist and a proponent of the same values that were most important to us. In the 1994 election, she ran for Governor of Maryland. She actually won the office, or should I say, at least she had the most votes until the City of Baltimore reported putting Democrat Parris Glendenning slightly ahead. Baltimore City somehow found thousands of extra votes. It didn't matter to them that the total number of votes was more than the number of legal registered voters and that the majority of these extra votes were "cemetery voters."

Voter identification is not required in Maryland. Sue had been a poll worker that year and was instructed by state officials in charge that it was illegal to ask for identification regardless of the circumstances. Sauerbrey sued, but the circuit court judge dismissed her case. Shortly after the inauguration of Governor Glendenning, he appointed that same judge to the Court of Special Appeals. This huge promotion I'm sure was just a coincidence.

In the spring of 2000, Sue and I had discussed whether we should again become active in politics, but we realized it wasn't in our personal best interest. We had already given up so much time and I wanted to get back to work. Things were once again going very well for us. Our commercial lending business continued to grow. Our income had increased and our net worth had climbed rapidly to an even higher eight figure amount. Since my successful operation at Johns Hopkins Hospital, my health had improved more than me or anyone else had expected.

Despite my reluctance, it was too difficult not to become politically involved as we were getting so many unfavorable reports regarding one of the commissioners we endorsed. Gouge surprised everyone when she teamed up with Democrat Governor Glendenning and supported his Smart Growth agenda. Even more shocking was her vote against the Rash's golf course development proposal which she had promised faithfully to support. When the other two commissioners outvoted her in favor of it, Gouge wrote a strong dissenting opinion supporting the governor's anti-growth policies and encouraged an anti-development group to file a lawsuit to stop the project. Gouge and her anti-growth supporters won the lawsuit on the technicality that the county had not followed all of the proper zoning procedures.

Gouge betrayed her close friend Eddie Rash, and all of the farmers for that matter, to advance her political career by gaining the support of the new anti-growth movement occurring in the southern part of the county. They were mostly large numbers of new citizens who had moved from the surrounding urban areas in the past few years and wanted to put a stop to any new residential development. Eddie expressed to me the pain he suffered from her betrayal and soon after died without ever realizing any of his dreams or benefits from his property.

I was getting reports regularly, now more than ever, of major corruption at the county office building involving this one commissioner. These accusations were not from Gouge's opponents, but from high-level, credible employees within the administration. They implied everything from huge cash payoffs for development favors to large amounts of money being funneled from the county's airport directly to this commissioner.

Seeking advice about what I should do, I called my friend Peter Scop and told him what was going on in our county government. Peter and I had discussed politics many times and he was not only the smartest person I knew, but he also had been personally familiar with many serious political situations himself. I told him I was shocked at the corruption going on in Carroll County politics. Peter actually laughed and told me I was very naïve.

He said my county was not unlike many other counties throughout the country. He cited similar situations he was aware of in New Jersey and Massachusetts.

"Unless you're into pain, stay out of it," Peter said.

That made sense and I took his advice, at least for the time being.

Of course, Stu, the liberal editor, continued to accuse me of influencing the commissioners for every decision they made that he was in disagreement with even though I had not spoken to either of the commissioners on any of those issues. Usually, I wasn't even aware of what the issues were as I had been doing my best to stay out of politics altogether and just run my lending business. There were regular columns and letters to the editor in the county newspaper blaming me for everything from the installation of radio towers to new road construction. There were even several stories reporting that I was financing the builders of all new residential development throughout the county.

I told Stu several times, I adhered to a very strict policy of not financing any businesses in the county. He knew that was true because all of my loans were public record; it wasn't as if he had to take my word for it, but that didn't matter to him. He just kept on printing the same old fabrications.

Almost every day, he had columns and editorials unfairly, and dishonestly, criticizing Dell and Frazier, the two decent county commissioners. He covered up or simply didn't report the corruption by Gouge and her cronies because she held to his liberal philosophies.

Before these experiences, I would have never believed this sort of thing happened anywhere in this country, but this was only the beginning of a repulsive political education I would ultimately receive. Sue and I soon learned it wasn't just in our county, but as Peter had told me, it was throughout the country and at every level of politics. Even so, learning of the corruption in our county office building was very upsetting, as was the constant ridicule by the liberal press of the two honest commissioners while defending and protecting the corrupt one. Nevertheless, I desperately wanted to stay out of politics, but it was not meant to be.

After the 2000 Presidential Election, there was quite a to-do over the Florida ballots that made the term "hanging chad," infamous. Who could

ever forget that? Both sides were claiming victory and the case was headed
for the U. S. Supreme Court.

I received a call from Ellen Sauerbrey requesting I assemble as many
people as I could to attend a rally on behalf of Republican candidate and
former Governor George W. Bush in Washington. She said the democrats
were sending their union supporters to a rally for Democrat candidate Al
Gore to be held directly across the street from the vice president's residence
on Massachusetts Avenue. Ellen felt it was important for us to have a conservative representation there. Sue and I spent the evening calling members
of the association asking them to attend the rally.

The following day, several hundred conservative Republicans from
Maryland and Virginia arrived; all with handmade signs supporting George
W. Bush. In contrast, the Democrats had about 50 people on the other side
of the street. That night on each Washington local news broadcast the media showed close-ups of a few Democrats on one side of the street and
close-up shots of a few Republicans on the other side of the street making
it appear as if there was no difference in the size of each group. This was
my first hands-on experience of a behind-the-scene look at the obvious bias
in the media. While filming the rally, a woman I didn't know told me she
was with Dick Cheney's office and wanted my name and telephone number
which I gladly gave her.

A day or two later, I received a call from someone with the campaign
asking if I could go to Florida and form a similar rally to support Bush as
Jesse Jackson was planning a huge rally supporting Gore. I only had a day's
notice, but I locked up the house and Sue and I flew directly from our farm
to West Palm Beach. We spent the evening calling different Republican
clubs requesting they get as many Bush supporters as they could to attend
the rally the next day. The same thing happened in West Palm Beach that
occurred in Washington. We had many times more Bush supporters then
did Jackson for Gore. I believe what upset Jackson more than anything else
was that many of the Bush supporters were African-Americans all holding
up handmade signs in support of Bush. I spoke briefly with Jackson and
tried to be pleasant but I could plainly see he was very angry about the
Republican opposition.

I flew home the next day feeling satisfied that we had actually accomplished our mission. I truly thought this would probably be the end of our involvement. Wrong again. Just a few days later, I received a call from an official with the Bush-Cheney team. He asked if we would be willing to volunteer our services at the temporary offices that had been opened in McLean, Virginia for the Bush-Cheney transition. I don't believe George W. Bush had even been declared the winner yet. When we arrived, there were only a few people at the newly opened temporary location. The person in charge of the volunteers, Jeanie Figg, knew that we were on the list to be there, but didn't know what assignments were meant for us. Sue worked in the office with Jeanie and I spent the next few days just going from office to office helping with whatever needed to be done.

My friend Alan called and asked me what I was doing there. When I told him he said, "It sounds to me that you're just the go-fer."

"Oh no Alan, you're wrong, the go-fer's my boss."

Three or four days later, I was told Vickers Meadows wanted to see me in her office at once. She had been with Bush for a very long time and was in charge of the transition team. I assumed I was in trouble for something I had done, but when I arrived at her office that wasn't the case at all. She told me she wanted to remove me as a volunteer and put me on as a staff member. She wanted to assign me and one other volunteer, Jim Henley, a person I had become very fond of, to pick up the cabinet nominees as they arrived at the airport: get them set up in their local hotels; and facilitate many of their needs until they were confirmed by Congress; at which point the Secret Service would take over. The only hitch she said was that I might need a security clearance and if so, it wouldn't be possible as a clearance of this nature could take quite some time.

When I left her office, I immediately called agent Truman and explained the situation to him. He told me if a clearance was necessary to have her call him. He believed he could have whatever she needed taken care of immediately. That night it was snowing very hard and I learned that Jeanie had to pick up somebody at Reagan National Airport. I had a four-wheel drive vehicle and volunteered to take her. Sue, Jeanie and I all went to the airport that night. I told Jeanie of my conversation with the bureau and

I was sure they would provide whatever was required. While sitting with Jeanie that same night, I received two telephone calls; first from a good friend who happened to be a judge on the Court of Appeals, the other from another very good friend, Congressman Roscoe Bartlett. Both were curious to know how things were going at the transition. I still remember Jeanie looking at me askance. I told her the truth; I was only a nobody and just thrilled to be there.

Soon, I was accommodating all the cabinet nominees. When Dr. Condoleezza Rice arrived late one night at Dulles Airport, Sue went in to meet her as I waited in the car. Moments later Sue called me on my cell phone and said a man had approached them and was flailing and raising his voice at Dr. Rice, blaming her and Bush for all the worlds' problems. Sue was afraid he could become violent and positioned herself between the man and Dr. Rice. I drove directly across the sidewalk to meet them at the door. Sue was shaking and physically upset, but Dr. Rice was as calm as a cucumber. It didn't seem to bother her at all.

By the time we got Dr. Rice checked into her hotel and drove another hour and a half to get home it was past 1:00 a.m. I had to pick up Dr. Rice at 7:00 a.m. later that same morning, which meant I had to leave my house at 5:30 a.m. With less than four hours sleep I was very tired. Dr. Rice knew Washington like the back of her hand and was telling me shortcuts to get through DC traffic. Once, when she told me to turn right, I mistakenly turned left. I expected she would be upset, but all she did was smile. Sue and I were privileged to meet and spend time with her.

Gale Norton was nominated to become Secretary of Agriculture and Sue and I spent a considerable amount of our time getting to know her as well. She was an incredibly wonderful, down-to-earth person who the night before her confirmation by Congress, had dinner with us at a fast food restaurant.

John Ashcroft had been nominated Attorney General. He too treated Sue and me as if we were family. When he was Attorney General, I had written him a couple of letters and received a kind, personal response from him both times.

It seemed to me that if this were a Hollywood movie, most of President George W. Bush's appointments had come directly from a great casting director. The President seemed to have a talent for choosing the nicest and most competent people for each position, at least most of the time.

The first several weeks in McLean, Sue and I had the time of our lives. A month or so before the inauguration, the entire operation was moved to G Street in Washington about a block from the White House. Things became very hectic and many more people had to be employed. Dozens of people were coming in every day. Sue worked in the welcome center and I continued my normal duties while looking forward to Inauguration Day when, after having such a great experience, we would finally be able to stay home, relax and take care of our business.

Most people that worked at the transition were looking for positions in the administration. When Sue and I were asked what positions we were seeking, our answer was always, "None."

We had taken off about three months; it was time for us to get back to work. The memories we have of our incredible experience are priceless, not to mention the thousands of pictures I had taken. I always had my camera with me and had often been asked to take many official pictures at the transition as well as the honor of taking and assembling an official Bush-Cheney Transition Team Album.

After the inauguration, most people left transition headquarters on G Street. Sue and I were asked to stay on for a while. I was cleaning up old files and Sue was helping set up the White House Social Office in for the new Social Secretary, Cathy Fenton, and, now Deputy Social Secretary, Jeanie Figg.

On the way home one night, Sue told me she had been offered a job in the White House. She told them she and I agreed not to accept any position as we had to get back to work in our own business. I asked her what job they offered her.

"A position in the social office."

"That's not a job, it's a party. You have to accept it. You will have the time of your life."

"Cathy and Jeanie are two of the most wonderful people we have ever known and had the privilege of working with. What a great opportunity it would be for you. How could you possibly turn that down?"

Sue had worked with me since she was 20-years old and was a little nervous about accepting this position. The next morning, she proudly called me from her desk in the social office at the White House. Sue knew they were working with a limited budget; she made it clear she would not accept a salary and would only work as a full-time volunteer.

Within a couple of days, Jeanie called and suggested I help with the events. She said the people in the president's cabinet had gotten to know Sue and me and were comfortable with us. I loved Jeanie, and as important as she was I was touched by her concern about someone as unimportant to the administration as me. It couldn't have been more perfect; Sue full-time in the social office, me participating with the social events.

The drive to the White House during rush hour took about an hour and a half. Sue left every morning shortly after 6:00 a.m. and seldom returned home before 7:00 p.m. It meant I was now doing all of Sue's work in our commercial lending business but that was a small sacrifice. Sue was proud to be working in the Bush White House and loved working with Cathy and Jeanie. I had never known her to be so happy. Sue also became the voice of the White House. When you called the main number of the White House you were greeted with a recorded voice message by Sue thanking you for calling and directing you to the appropriate agency.

In Sue's first week, she received an invitation from first lady Laura Bush inviting her staff to coffee in the private residence. When Sue came home she was so excited to tell me of her experience. Mrs. Bush had actually opened the door and held it open for her and the staff so that they could walk out onto the balcony to view the Washington Monument and the Jefferson Memorial. Sue could not believe that the first lady, herself, actually opened and held the door for them. She was also so impressed that Mrs. Bush's main concern was that her staff members who had relocated from other parts of the country had satisfactorily settled in.

About 10:00 p.m. one night, I had just completed an event with Sue. It was thrilling. I was in the Lower Cross Hall of the White House with Karl Rove. In jest, I asked Karl to pretend to be vacuuming so I could take a picture and show my friends what he did at the White House. To my surprise, he actually took the upright vacuum cleaner and he and Jeanie vacuumed the floor as I took pictures.

Somebody came by and said it was snowing outside and I said I had to go because I was parked several blocks away. The next day, I was scheduled to work another event. Sue called to tell me when I came in that evening to pull directly up to the East Gate. When I arrived the guard opened the gate and I was directed to the second of three checkpoints. Upon pulling up to the second checkpoint, I was further directed through the area where most of the high level White House employees park. Arriving at the third entrance, the gate was opened and I was directed to a park in a small area only a few feet from the entrance to the White House. I was permitted to park there not only on that night, but for all of the more than the 100 events I worked over the next six years.

Sue loved her work at the White House and I was more than content spending my days concentrating primarily on our commercial lending business which continued to do well. On the second Tuesday of September 2001, I attended a breakfast at my Bonds Meadow Rotary club in Westminster, Maryland. After the meeting, I stood outside talking with a good friend who was a financial advisor. He was telling me how pleased he was with the direction the country was going. He believed the economy was on the right track and told me how well his business was doing. While we were talking, I could hear the phone in my car ringing, but I was enjoying my conversation and just ignored it. Within a few minutes it rang again, and again. I knew something important must have happened as nobody called me continuously that early in the morning. When I answered the phone, it was Sue. She was screaming and almost unintelligible. I could tell she was running and almost out of breath. She said something about our country being attacked and that she and the others were running out of the White House. She said the Secret Service was everywhere, armed with their machine guns. I asked if she was alright and she said yes. I asked if the President was okay and she said she was terrified and didn't know. She told me not to come into Washington because all the roads in every direction were jammed with cars at a standstill. Nothing was moving and it was impossible to get into or out of the city. She said everyone was afraid to take the metro subway as it could also be a target of an attack.

People were running in every direction not knowing where to go or what to do. Many were running toward the Ellipse but she and the others from the social office did not want to be near the Washington Monument for fear that it too could be a target. She said they would figure out where to go and call me back.

Both my friend and I raced to our homes. This was to become the most terrible day of my life. I had never felt so much pain and terror as I watched on television the collapsing of the twin towers in New York. I seldom remember ever crying in my entire life, but when I saw the airplane crash and explode into the Pentagon and learned that Barbara Olson was on that flight, it was impossible to control myself and the tears poured down my face. I knew and loved Barbara and had just recently received a letter from her thanking me for some pictures I had taken of her.

Sue called me several times that day, but she was unable to arrive home until later that night. All we could do was cry and pray together.

I sent the pictures I had taken of Barbara to her husband, Ted Olson. A couple of days later, he called me at my home. Even in a time of such tragedy and grief, he took the time to thank me and say how the pictures meant so much to him. He also told me that John Ashcroft wanted one of them so he could look at it every day to remind himself of how much we all had lost.

At the memorial service it was said that Barbara loved country music and her favorite song was "The Dance," by Garth Brooks. Who could have ever expected that the lyrics in the song she loved so much, written by the brilliant Tony Astrata, would apply so poignantly to her and in a way that no one could have ever imagined. I sealed in plastic a few verses from that song and I carry it with me even to this day. It reminds me how evil the terrorists are and how much we all lost that day.

I'd like to share them with you:

> "Looking back on the memory of
> The dance we shared 'neath the stars above
> For a moment all the world was right
> How could I have known that you'd ever say goodbye
> And now I'm glad I didn't know
> The way it all would end, the way it all would go
> Our lives are better left to chance

I could have missed the pain
But I'd of had to miss the dance"

Chapter 19
Selfless And Noble

A FEW DAYS later, I received a call from my cousin who lived and worked in New York City. She had always been very liberal and was a huge Gore supporter. She told me she couldn't believe she would ever say this, but on the night of the attack she thanked God that George Bush was our President.

After 9/11 a lot of people were reassessing their priorities and Sue was no exception. Between the campaign, transition, and her duties at the White House, Sue had been absent from our business for over a year. We agreed it was time for her to cut back, but both of us would continue to do the special events at the White House. Our official primary duty at the events we worked was to greet the guests and make sure we had their correct name and address so the photographs taken of them with the President and Mrs. Bush could be lined up with the proper identification cards. The White House photographer always took the official photographs. Sue and I would tell each guest that we would be at the event and if they needed anything at all to bring it to our attention. From the very first event we worked, Cathy and Jeanie had stressed to us how important it was to them that we do everything we could to ensure each guest had a wonderful and memorable experience.

The very first event I worked, I took a lot of pictures of many of the White House full-time employees including the wait staff. The next day, when I went in, they were all thrilled to receive the 8x10 photographs I had printed for them. One elderly, African-American man's eyes welled up with tears as he received his picture and told me he had been working at the White House for more than 40 years and never had his picture taken there. He repeatedly thanked me as if I had given him something far more valuable than just a photograph. I told Andi Ball, chief of staff for Mrs. Bush, about the reaction I received from the employees and she said it was very nice and encouraged me to continue.

Andi was a very strict, hard-working, competent woman but she was also a very nice and compassionate person. After that, I always had my camera with me and took photos at every event. It wasn't long before several officials were referring to me as the unofficial photographer at the White House. I had the exact same professional camera and lenses that were used by the official White House photographer and I used only state of the art printing equipment. Every year I took the group pictures of the military aides and band, and several other official groups and often received medallion medals in appreciation.

At many events guests would ask me to take a picture of them, sometimes in a preferred scene or with their favorite cabinet member. I always made it clear I was just a volunteer, but I also made it clear I was thrilled to be able to do it. I always sent them an 8x10 photograph and every single time I received back a kind thank you letter. Often they were guests I didn't know, but quite often they were senators, congressmen and well known celebrities. Regardless, they all loved being at the White House and getting their picture taken with the President and Mrs. Bush.

I was very well aware that among people's most prized possessions were their photographs. The fact that I could help preserve their memories at these important events meant as much to me as it did to them. In the six years I worked as a volunteer with the administration, I took over 65,000 pictures. It's been more than seven years since Sue or I have been in the White House, but I occasionally still get requests for photographs I had taken back then.

We worked many different White House events but nothing was as thrilling as the Christmas parties. Each year we would personally get to meet and greet every one of the thousands of attending guests. It was incredibly exciting to meet, in person, the very people we had seen in the movies and on television. Fox & Friends hosts Steve Doocy and Brian Kilmeade were even nicer and more personable than they were on television. Sean Hannity had an incredible personality and was a joy to talk to. Even most of the liberal press that had been criticizing the President, almost on a daily basis, were very polite and pleasant at the White House.

I say most, because there was one particular exception. He was a news person that came every year, and every year he was nastier than the year before. Of the thousands of guests that came to the White House, he was the only one that refused to hold his two-inch information card so his picture could be lined up with his name. He thought he was too important to do that. Every year I had to get a military aide to carry it for him. His criticisms, even while at the White House, were incredibly inappropriate. I don't think it proper for me to tell you who he was so I'll just make up a name, Chris Matthews.

I have to tell you one of the most interesting news anchors we met was Bill O'Reilly. He is nothing like the person you see on television. He was actually very modest and most humble. He was warm and exceptionally nice and he couldn't have been more gracious. It was also a pleasure meeting Tim Russert and so many others, both liberals and conservatives. Many had ideologies not consistent with the President's but you certainly would not have known it when they were guests at the White House.

There were a few that were really into their own self-importance. It was very interesting viewing some of the heated discussions between some anchor people within the same network. On one occasion I witnessed incredible dissension and bitterness between two very popular anchors that were on the same morning news show. Yet, watching them on television the next morning, you would think they were best of friends.

Most all of the movie celebrities were polite and very nice. A few were not and they made unfriendly, crude remarks. When I handed the information card to a very popular award-winning actress who had openly criticized the President, she looked at it and said, "I see you have my home address. Is that so if I do something wrong you know where to get me?"

I wanted to say, "No, we have it so if you surprise us and do something nice we will know where to send the thank you card." Though of course I didn't, I just smiled and told her to have a good time.

One of my all-time most favorite actresses is Shirley Jones. I told her I had watched the movie "Elmer Gantry" several times and how much I enjoyed her performance. She was exceptionally gracious and said it was one of her favorite roles and told me how excited she was to be at the White House. I was most surprised by my favorite actor. He was not very nice, in fact, quite obnoxious, and caused a woman on the wait staff to leave the room in tears. Thankfully, he was a rare exception. The overwhelming majority of the Hollywood crowd was very courteous and respectful, regardless of their political leanings.

Hollywood and news people were not the only people we met. More exciting to me was seeing all the senators and congressmen, many of whom we admired very much. By the end of our second year we knew just about all of them well enough not to have to ask their name. Never would I have expected to have ever been able to meet and talk to so many people we admired and respected so much; such as my absolute favorite justice on the Supreme Court.

Sue and I received so many other great benefits working there. Sue will always cherish the memory of the surprise birthday party they had for her. We were privileged to be present at the Kennedy Center Honors Awards, performances at Ford's Theatre, and many other great events the President and Mrs. Bush attended.

By far though the best benefit was getting to know the President and Mrs. Bush themselves. They were unlike so many other politicians we knew. Everyone always felt comfortable being around them because they never acted as if their position made them any more important than anyone else. I learned a lot about the President and Mrs. Bush from many of the career employees at the White House. Everyone there loved them both, which wasn't true about some of the other Presidents and first ladies. One of the young African-American waiters told me the President had taken him fishing at his ranch in Texas and I enjoyed hearing many funny stories of his experiences.

On many Sunday afternoons, President Bush would return by helicopter from Camp David to the South Lawn of the White House where he would find Sue and me with some of our conservative friends we had brought with us waiting to greet him. He was always very cordial and acted as if he were as glad to meet them as they were to meet him. One Sunday, we took Commissioner Robin Frazier and when she was introduced she whispered to him, "I pray for you every night." He smiled and continued to greet other people and proceeded to enter the South Entrance of the White House. He stopped, turned around and walked back to Robin and whispered, "I want to thank you for praying for me."

One evening after an event, Sue and I were finishing up in the Lower Cross Hall at about 11:00 p.m. We thought we were alone and were surprised when the President and Mrs. Bush walked into the hallway. They looked as surprised to see us at that hour as we were to see them. President Bush said, "I can't believe you're still here. I have to get a picture of this."

"No Mr. President, I can see how tired both of you are."

He insisted and called for a photographer. Sue and I have many official photographs with the President and Mrs. Bush, but the picture taken that night is the one we cherish the most. The President and Mrs. Bush both understood how meaningful the photograph would be and went out of their way to see that even the least important people were not left out.

On another evening, after the final Christmas party of the season, the President assembled the head usher, Gary Walters, with several of the White House residence staff and had pictures taken with them all wearing cowboy hats. Mrs. Bush and both of their daughters all participated. I was privileged being there and to have taken those photos. Many of the staff later told me that no other President had ever been so kind to them.

I had also gotten to know President George H. W. Bush and Mrs. Barbara Bush. I was the volunteer photographer at many of their charitable events. At one event, Barbara Bush said, "The person that treats you nice, but doesn't treat the waitress nice, is not a nice person." All of the Bush family had that same sense of decency and humility. Doro Bush Koch, President George W. Bush's sister, was the founder of The Maryland Family Literacy Initiative. She worked tirelessly for months every year on a major event in Maryland, "A Celebration of Reading," which has raised millions for the Barbara Bush Foundation for Family Literacy.

I didn't agree with every decision President Bush had made, but never doubted that he made them only because he absolutely believed that it was in the best interest of the country and for no other reason. I have personally known many Democrats that strongly disagreed with some of his policies, but even they knew of his love of America and never once questioned his loyalty. Most people will never know what a selfless and noble family they were in our White House; but I thank God I was somehow given the opportunity to discover it firsthand.

Chapter 20
Just When You Think You've Won

OTHER THAN THE limited work we did at the White House, our commercial lending business was keeping us pretty busy. The doctors at Johns Hopkins Hospital were concerned about new growths and lesions found on both of my kidneys but said nothing could be done at this time. By now I had learned that if "nothing could be done," I should just ignore those types of reports. My life was better than I could have ever imagined. If it weren't for the constant negative press I was getting in a local county newspaper, everything would have been perfect. Editor Stu believed I had too much conservative influence in county politics. He wanted me out and I wanted little more than to stay out, but it really was difficult as so many people were soliciting me to do something about the corruption of that one commissioner.

I was invited to attend a breakfast event for a local congressman sponsored by a Baltimore law firm. He wasn't my congressman, but I was a friend of an attorney in the firm so I agreed to attend. His name was Robert Ehrlich. He gave a superb speech denouncing the culture of corruption in Maryland and was adamant in his belief that it could be stopped. I was so inspired by his words, I told him he should run for governor. He said he had thought about it, but didn't believe it was possible for a Republican to win in this liberal state. It hadn't been done in over 35 years. I strongly disagreed. Ehrlich was young, attractive and spoke eloquently; his stand against corruption made him the perfect candidate, at least for me. I told him if he would run I could get many major influential Democrats to support him and I would be very active on his campaign finance committee. He asked me to name one Democrat that would support him and I gave him the name of one of the most influential Democrats in the state. He said he couldn't believe it. A few days later that Democrat and I had a meeting in the congressman's office in Washington and he assured Ehrlich of his strong support.

I could hardly control my excitement when Robert Ehrlich ultimately agreed to run for the office of governor. It was not difficult for me to convince several other prominent Democrats to also support his candidacy.

At the time I didn't personally know Dick Hug, but I knew of his reputation as being one of the country's best fundraisers. I was excited that he had agreed to chair the finance committee. I was pleased to be on that committee and also agreed to personally take all the pictures and print photographs at every event. When Ehrlich officially announced on March 15, 2002, that he was running for the office of governor opposing the current, very well-known and popular Lieutenant Governor, Kathleen Kennedy Townsend, we all knew it would be an uphill battle, but he was determined and so was I.

I was willing to do anything I could to help Bob Ehrlich get elected. I was photographing every event whether they were breakfast or lunch meetings or fundraising events usually held in the evening and on weekends. People would anxiously wait in long lines to have their picture taken with him. Sometimes I would spend the entire day with Ehrlich photographing events from early in the morning to late in the evening. Often I would get home after 10 or 11 o'clock; then I would stay up until two or three in the morning printing the pictures so the campaign could send them out the following day. Often the very next day I would do it all over again. In addition to taking thousands of campaign photographs as well as printing them, I attended every finance committee meeting and we raised a lot of money. In fact, the finance committee exceeded our goals and raised far more money for a Republican candidate than had ever been raised in this state before. At the same time, Sue and I worked many events at the White House and we still had to manage our loan business.

As if I didn't have enough on my plate, included on the ballot in the upcoming election was the election of our three county commissioners. I was under constant pressure from several local attorneys and business professionals to throw my hat in the ring to run for county commissioner, but I thought under no circumstances would I ever consider it. A few months before the election and just before the deadline to register as a candidate, I learned a questionable development group had committed to support the one corrupt commissioner we wanted desperately out of office as well as two new candidates that were absolute buffoons. I believed they knew they could easily control these three. At that point, I succumbed to the pressure and registered as a candidate for county commissioner. I learned that when one of the buffoons was told of my candidacy said, "Why is Primoff running? He doesn't need a job."

Most of my supporters knew I wasn't really running to become a commissioner at all. I couldn't give up my business. I was running only to try to keep the crooks out of office. With all of the constant bias negative press, I didn't think it was possible to win, but if by some chance I did, I would not have served very long. I would have resigned with the full confidence that the Carroll County Republican Central Committee would have chosen a very good conservative replacement that would have pleased my supporters.

The happiest person in the county about my candidacy was Editor Stu who now had a real target to go after, but he wasn't the only one. Other liberal publications in the county also printed many erroneous articles. Stu however, led the pack and was now more relentless than ever. Almost every day, he would have fallacious articles and editorials about me. Sue was on the county ethics commission and he also fabricated many dishonest stories about her and the other two ethics commission members. We were experiencing on a county level the same thing President Bush was experiencing by the liberal national media.

Stu and other liberal newspapers printed articles and letters to the editor that enraged many Carroll County citizens. Before a county meeting, as I was standing outside talking with some of our association members, a man wearing a backpack, appearing to be about 30 years-old, approached me. The veins in his neck were popping with anger as he told me he knew who I was and said I was destroying the county and our environment by financing all the current residential development. He said I deserved what he was going to do to me and I should enjoy my life, that is, what I had left before he finished me off.

I took it seriously as did the other people that heard him. He walked away and left the area. He intentionally had not parked in the parking lot, clearly so we could not get his license plate. I was unaware that a woman who had heard his threats told her daughter to follow him and she did get his license plate number.

The next day I filed a police report. I received a call from the assigned police officer who just so happened to be someone who knew me. He told me the man was an environmentalist who didn't have a job and was living off of his parents. The man told him he was upset about all the things he had read in the newspaper concerning me. He believed I was totally responsible for destroying the county by financing all of the new project developments. The policeman told him he knew me personally and what he had read in the newspaper was not true, that I did not do any business in Carroll County whatsoever.

The officer said the man was very surprised and wanted to come to my house to apologize. I said I would drop the charges and asked him to tell the man to just leave me alone.

I called editor Stu and asked him to call the policeman so he could hear for himself how much danger he was causing me. His tart and unconcerned response was; "I can't be responsible for every nut out there."

One particular person had more letters to the editor in the newspaper about me than anyone else. His name was Nolan David and his letters were the ugliest of all. I couldn't believe that one of the newspapers published a letter from him that stated I had flown into Carroll County on my private jet from the very liberal Prince George's County with a bag full of gelt. He said I was running the county government from my living room. I had not moved to Carroll County from Prince George's County at all. Before purchasing my farm I had lived in adjacent Howard County for almost 20 years and it was very obvious why he chose the phrase, "bag full of gelt." I certainly had not been running the county, nor did I ever own a jet.

After that letter was published David received a telephone call from a man named Mr. Smith who said he had read his letters in the newspaper and wanted to help expose me as someone destroying our county. David told him he and someone working at the newspaper were on a campaign to destroy any influence I could have in this county. Over the course of several months Smith developed a strong telephone friendship with David and eventually asked him if he actually knew me.

David boasted he knew me very well and said he had even been to Primoff's house and had breakfast with me more than once. David said I was really an exceptionally nice person and nothing they were writing about me was really the truth, but he and the others had an agenda and I was a very easy target.

The person to whom Mr. David had made these admissions was a private detective that I had hired. He converted his conversations into a final report which he provided to me. It is difficult for a public figure to take any action against anyone publishing even false statements, but I have the report available if Mr. David would like to read it and embarrass himself.

Other people in this unscrupulous group published stories on the Internet, going so far as to claim I was a member of the Ku Klux Klan. One such internet article stated they had acquired unquestionable documentation that I was a registered member of the Nazi Party. There was no limit as to how low these people will go to destroy the credibility of anyone whose ideologies they oppose.

Several times I would arrive home only to find my driveway filled with broken glass. Becoming involved in politics had given me a lesson in life I never could have ever imagined.

One evening I was leaving a county meeting that was attended by the local press. I heard in the shadows a voice saying, "Psst, psst, Mr. Primoff, come here please." It was dark and I admit I was frightened, but as I looked into the darkness I recognized a young reporter that worked for the liberal newspaper. When I approached her I could see she was very nervous. She said she would lose her job if it was discovered she had this conversation but felt compelled to tell me something. She said that her editor, Stu, had told her and the other young reporters that if they wanted to advance at the newspaper they had to get dirt on Ed Primoff. Apparently he didn't care if it was true or not. "I don't know what he has against you, but I thought you needed to know."

I thanked her profusely for having the courage to tell me, but said not to let it upset her. I told her she had far too much character to work for this sleazy publication. In a very short time, she was no longer with the newspaper.

More than a year after she was gone, I was having a meeting with Stu and without disclosing her identity I told him what I had heard from one of his reporters. He thought it was funny and said he knew who it probably was and he was glad to get rid of her.

Stu knew, and I think was proud of the grief caused by the fictitious articles. What he did not know however was the personal pain I was suffering when my young 52 year old sister had a heart attack and died during my campaign and only months after my mother passed away. Although I believe he would not have cared or altered his conduct in any way.

A few weeks before the election one of my most avid supporters called about something she had read in the newspaper. She said she had ignored all the outrageous reports about me but this particular article stated that when I was on the planning commission it was unconscionable that I voted to rezone my own property. She still supported me she said, but thought it would have been wise for me to have recused myself at the time the vote was taken. Further, she felt the article was very damaging to my candidacy.

She was absolutely astonished when I told her I was never on the planning commission, and that I never requested or received a zoning change on my property. She was flabbergasted that any publication would print such false statements. I told her it really didn't matter as I had not been putting very much effort into winning the commissioner's race and she shouldn't either. It was far more important to put all of our effort into the governor's race. She was a great help at probably the largest and most successful private fundraiser ever held for Bob Ehrlich which we hosted on my farm and attended by almost 1,000 people.

In July 2002, there was a large rally in Annapolis where Ehrlich made the announcement that he had chosen Michael Steele to run as his lieutenant governor. Reporters from the *Washington Post, The Baltimore Sun*, and many other newspapers were represented to cover the event. I was photographing Bob and Michael at the podium when a reporter approached and asked if I was the campaign's official photographer. When I answered I was, he asked what I thought of Michael Steele. "I think he was a great choice."

"But what do you think about ... well, you know?"

"What do you mean, 'You know?'"

"You know, what do you think about the fact that he picked a black candidate to run with him?"

I looked at him surprisingly and said, "Michael Steele is black? I hadn't noticed."

He smiled and said, "Touché."

I had no doubt that Bob Ehrlich could not have picked a better running-mate. In the months to come, Sue and I gained great respect for Michael Steele. He is conservative and an articulate speaker and has an incredible ability to motivate people far better than most politicians. He is a genuinely nice person which makes it very easy for people to like him. He also has skin thick enough to handle the constant criticisms that African-American conservative politicians receive. He shrugged off the comments made by Maryland Democrat Senate President Mike Miller referring to him as an "Uncle Tom" and the constant assaults such as being pelted with Oreo cookies at an event during a debate at Morgan State University in Baltimore. I whole heartily believe because of the way he skillfully handled those attacks, they actually helped him and the campaign.

The month before the election, Sue and I worked relentlessly seven days a week on the governor's race. We were now more motivated than ever as polls were indicating Ehrlich could actually win. Events were scheduled even more frequently and closer together. I was literally taking and printing thousands of pictures from the events and fundraisers every week. Sue and I were both so tired and relieved the campaign was finally coming to an end.

Just before the election we thought we were done, but were told that Ehrlich and Steele were going to campaign by walking door-to-door in Prince George's County in the morning and in Montgomery County in the afternoon and they wanted photos taken. We met them in Prince George's County on that very cold morning. We walked for several hours and took photographs of them conversing with the prospective voters.

Early that afternoon we reassembled in Montgomery County. It had become very windy and seemed a lot colder. Before we started our door-to-door walk, Ehrlich put his arms together across his chest and indicated to me he was very cold. He was not wearing a coat. I took off a new double-wide cashmere scarf that Sue had given me for our anniversary and handed it to him. The walk was on a downhill slope that was about a half mile long so it was easier than the walk we had done that morning.

We finished late in the afternoon when it had become considerably colder. As we finished and arrived at the bottom of the hill, Ehrlich's SUV pulled up and he got in and was driven away. Sue and I were surprised and disappointed we were left at the bottom of the hill to walk all the way back in the cold weather carrying all of our heavy camera equipment.

We had been with him since early that morning; surely he knew how tired and cold we were. He didn't even take time to return my cashmere scarf. This was completely unlike the Ehrlich we had gotten to know. However, didn't take it personally because we realized he had not received as warm of a reception as any of us had expected in both Prince George's and Montgomery County. We understood that he was consumed with worry and with good cause.

By a squeaker, Robert Ehrlich and Michael Steele won the election. Sue and I felt privileged enjoying the celebration in his private room that night with many of his major supporters and close friends from his college days until late into the night.

In the Carroll County Commissioner race, out of the 18 people that ran, I received more votes than anyone else, that is with the exception of the three who won. These were the same three candidates those particular developers I previously told you about, had spent a huge amount of money and effort supporting. Most people in the county had no idea of the level of corruption that would take place in the coming years.

One of the first actions taken by these commissioners was to sell a county owned property in Hampstead. It was a large brick schoolhouse on approximately five acres that was vacant and no longer needed. I, along with several other businessmen, expected it would sell for $1 to $2 million; revenue that would be added to the county treasury. The recorded contract of sale dated March 6, 2003 and recorded July 25, 2003, in book 3359, page

0051, stated that the total purchase price to be paid by the buyer was one dollar. That's not a misprint; it actually states $1.00. The subsequent recorded deed dated June 21, 2004, in book 4045, page 0669, reported that in fact the consideration paid was actually $1.00.

These same commissioners also purchased, with taxpayer dollars, several real estate properties. I believed the purchase price far exceeded their actual values. The county had paid almost $2 million for one of these properties. It was unused and remained vacant for several years and was ultimately sold for a fraction of what the county paid, leaving the taxpayers with an incredible loss. I'm quite sure though that the developers who supported these three commissioners were very pleased with their investment.

Commissioner Gouge, one of the three candidates supported by the development group, after being re-elected, remained the president of the board. She was concerned about a serious corruption complaint from a private citizen against her that the ethics commission had been investigating for several months. The complaint alleged that she had strong-armed a local businessman to install a driveway for her daughter at a price that was less than his actual cost. It took incredible courage for the owner of the paving company, Charles Stambaugh, to file this complaint as his company did a substantial amount of work for the county.

The ethics commission investigated the accusations of the tactics of Gouge. A complaint was never made or investigated against her daughter as she was not a county employee. The authority of the ethics commission extends only to county employees; certainly not private citizens. However, in an effort to take the spotlight off of Gouge, editor Stu wrote outright dishonest articles criticizing the ethics commission for investigating Gouge's daughter.

Gouge knew if the ethics commission report was finalized and released, she would be exposed. Her response was swift and simple. She had the other two new commissioners vote with her and fired the entire ethics commission before their report could be completed and released.

The chairman of the ethics commission, Reverend James Talley, was one of the most highly respected ministers in the county and was outraged over the firing and untrue accusations against the ethics commission. He took it personally and suffered a severe heart attack, but thankfully recovered. John Harner, a man of unquestionable character, was the other member of the ethics commission. He was retired from private industry and was a lifelong farmer and a charter member of the Harney Volunteer Fire Department. He was also the organist for his church and was very angry over the dishonest accusations and firing. A few short months later he died suddenly at the age of 79. His funeral was attended by more than 1,000 people.

The ethics commission sued the commissioners in an attempt to get their positions reinstated and enable them to complete and release their report to the public. Unfortunately, the court ruled that the law did permit the county commissioners to fire the ethics commission without justification of any kind. Their work product on this case was destroyed and never released.

Chapter 21
110 Million Reasons To Destroy
The U.S. Economy

ALTHOUGH I WAS disappointed with the results of our county election, we had succeeded with the far more important election; the governor's race. I believed I had come to know Robert Ehrlich extremely well. I had made a lot of new friends in statewide Republican circles as well as many important Democrats who had supported his candidacy. *The Baltimore Sun* had actually printed an article that stated the governor relied on me as one of his top advisers, which believe me, was never the case. Governor Ehrlich actually did a good job as governor, certainly much better than his predecessors. Yet, most of his major supporters including myself were very disappointed when he made the same mistake so many other Republicans make. He believed, in order to win a second term he had to move to the middle and acquiesce to the Democrats.

One of the first appointments Ehrlich made as governor was that of the Director of Assessments and Taxation to Bob Wolfing. He was the chairman of our Carroll County Republican Central Committee and was more than qualified for that position. He also worked tenaciously on the governor's campaign delivering an astounding 81 percent of Carroll's total vote for Ehrlich. After the official announcement in *The Baltimore Sun* and other newspapers, Wolfing sold his company in order to prepare for his new position. But just two days before he was to assume his new duties he was notified by the administration that the Democrats were putting extreme pressure on Ehrlich to appoint one of their own. At Wolfing's request I called Larry Hogan, the governor's appointment secretary, and was told he thought everything would be fine, just let things calm down. Two weeks later, we were surprised and quite disappointed to learn that the governor had withdrawn Wolfing's appointment and caved to the Democrat's choice.

Another appointment as a tax court judge was promised to Donald Messenger, an attorney who was a friend of the governor's and had also worked very hard on his election. I didn't know anyone who didn't love Messenger. Even the liberal *Baltimore Sun* apparently loved the conservative letters to the editor he submitted every month as they published them regularly.

Messenger spent his life in the service of others and was the most decent and honest attorney I had ever known. He had absolutely been assured of an appointment to that position on the condition that he would have to move into another jurisdiction. He and his wife despised the thought of relocating their residence, but he had taught tax law at a local university and always desired this position. After Messenger sold his home, he moved to a suburb of Annapolis. Without any notice to him, the governor appointed the candidate the Democrats had recommended instead.

Messenger was devastated. Later he developed cancer and just two weeks before his death last year, instead of talking about his terminal condition, he could only bring himself to remind me of what the governor had done to him and his family.

A third person who had also worked persistently on the governor's candidacy had given up his job managing a prestigious car dealership to accept the position to head the state's motor vehicle administration. The position paid less than half what he was making at the car dealership but he was dedicated and confident that he could fix the problems at the MVA. He was so proud when he came to my house and asked me to take and print his picture for *The Baltimore Sun* that would run the next day announcing his appointment. He had spent two weeks training his replacement at the car dealership and although he was going to make considerably less money, he was determined to fix the incompetence and long lines at the MVA.

Once again, after the announcement in the newspaper, this loyal Republican was notified the governor had succumbed to the pressures of the Democrats and let their candidate remain in office. The long lines and arrogant abuse by the government employees at the MVA continues to this day.

Over the next few months, I regularly received complaints about the governor's appointments. Many people had seen me throughout the election with Ehrlich and had read articles in *The Baltimore Sun*. They believed I had influence with the administration and were demanding I speak with him about appointments in their county, especially in the district and circuit court judge arena. One important county official in Maryland told me his county had never had a Republican judge in the two positions that were becoming available and they expected both of them to be filled with their Republican nominees. Unfortunately, they were not. The official called me back and asked me if this was the way the governor rewarded his county after they had voted overwhelmingly for him. He directed his anger at me for not using my so-called influence with the governor, as if I could have done something about it. He still holds me responsible.

Most of the judicial appointments throughout the state were filled by Democrats. Of course I spoke with Governor Ehrlich about these appointments several times. I had little influence but enjoyed a very good relationship with him. He was always very pleasant to us. I could gain nothing by alienating him. I knew with certainty he was irreparably harming himself and the result would be the loss of the next election which was troubling to all of us. When I did try to talk to him about his reelection possibilities his answer was always the same, "What are they going to do, vote for O'Malley, the Democrat?"

My response was also always the same, "No Bob, Republicans don't do that. They just won't vote." I refused several requests to participate in any way in his reelection campaign. He had alienated so many of the hard-working key people in the Maryland Republican Party, I was convinced he had no chance of winning a second term.

I sincerely wish I had been wrong, but unfortunately I was not. He lost by a landslide to O'Malley in an election he absolutely should have and could have easily won. It was one of the lowest Republican turnouts in

Maryland's history. He got under votes in every single county. Statewide, a large number of his supporters abandoned him by going to the polls to cast a vote for other offices and not for governor. He was also the only incumbent Republican Governor in the entire country who lost reelection that year, 2006.

Naturally Sue and I were distraught about Governor Ehrlich losing the race, but we were even more concerned about what was happening at the White House. After President Bush won his reelection in 2004 almost every secretary and cabinet member we knew had resigned as is almost always the case in every administration after the first term. There were so many people leaving that we respected and loved.

We also decided to give up working the events. Cathy Fenton, the President's social secretary personally asked us to continue on. She was leaving, but requested us to stay and help the new social secretary. Frankly, we had been determined to leave and would not have agreed to stay except that Cathy told us Anita McBride was going to become the new chief of staff for the first lady. We knew her and were extremely fond of Anita, both for her character and competence. We did stay, but became increasingly unhappy with a few of the new replacements. It had become a somewhat different White House with some of the new people concerned more with building their resumes rather than helping the President and first lady serve the country.

Even before the election, in 2003 I was puzzled why Scott McClellan was chosen to replace Ari Fleischer. I knew McClellan had been part of the Bush team for a very long time, but firmly believed that he was not always on the same page as the rest of the administration. Now that the 2004 election was over a small number of people like McClellan were replacing people like Fleischer. Sue and I couldn't imagine why, but we were worried about it.

We had loved doing the events and the people we worked with at the White House, but we came to the conclusion it had finally become time for us to retire our efforts in politics. When we were notified that summer of the upcoming winter schedule I replied that we wouldn't be able to accommodate them this season. We were told it was important for us to be there and were asked if we would just come to the White House to discuss it. When we arrived, both Sue and I felt badly as a special White House luncheon was prepared for us. After lunch we sat in Mrs. Bush's office with the new social secretary and explained some of the reasons why we couldn't continue, but never shared our real concerns.

Once again, it wasn't nearly as easy to stay completely out of county politics as we believed it would be. Before the election in 2006 we were constantly receiving requests to help do something about the abundance of corruption of our current three commissioners who were all running to be reelected and all were being supported by the liberal editor, Stu.

A couple of months before the election, we gave in and agreed to re-organize the Carroll County Republican Club to help oppose the current corrupt county administration. Scott Hollenbeck, a nurse by trade and a devoted patriot, was elected president and my wife Sue was elected secretary-treasurer. About 20 of the most politically concerned citizens in the county enrolled in the club's effort. We sought the counsel of two different prominent attorneys to make certain everything we did was absolutely legal as we realized if we were not successful there would be serious reprisals. Stu's newspaper refused most of our advertisements exposing the corruption of the three sitting commissioners, but other county newspapers, after vetting our documentation, did publish them.

We published government documents that absolutely contradicted what the commissioners were reporting. For example, knowing the liberal media would not challenge them, the sitting commissioners were running ads boasting that they had only increased the capital budget by six percent. The truth was that when they took office it was $27 million and they increased it to $110 million. When I went to school that would be a 400 percent increase, not six percent. That is not just misinformation, it's outright lying.

Almost all of their claims were similarly false. In another ad we published that a county employee had spent more than $1,200 for a deluxe oceanfront suite at taxpayer's expense. These figures were taken directly from the county records through a Freedom of Information request. The commissioners were outraged and pledged revenge.

All three received far fewer votes than they had gotten four years earlier. Because of their vulnerability I believe more people than ever ran for that office. In spite of the reduction in their votes, Julia Walsh Gouge and one other commissioner retained their office.

It was now time for their revenge. They demanded, along with some of their supporters, for the Maryland State Prosecutor to criminally prosecute us for the ads we had published. At first I thought it was a ridiculous joke, but soon learned they were very sincere.

I was soon contacted by Thomas M. McDonough of the state prosecutor's office. When my attorney and I met with McDonough he told us all he was looking for was for me to plead guilty and pay a fine and there would be no criminal prosecution. It was very apparent he thought this would be a very easy and quick case. He was only making this charge in order to satisfy our adversarial influential politicians by embarrassing us into a wrongful admission that we had broken the law. He became very upset when I told him there was no way we would plead guilty to a crime we didn't commit. He reminded me he had prosecuted Linda Tripp, infamous for recording a conversation with Monica Lewinsky, which involved President Clinton. I reminded him that he lost that case and told him that if he charged us he would lose this one as well. Over the next month or so we had several meetings with him. He literally begged me to plead guilty.

At the last meeting we had he said, "If you just plead guilty there will be no charge of any kind and no fine, please just plead guilty. If you don't, Scott Hollenbeck and your wife will be charged criminally and they could each be sentenced to two years in prison and ordered to pay fines of thousands of dollars."

I responded that I was against any plea, but would leave it up to Sue and Scott. After I notified him neither of them would plead guilty he officially charged both of them criminally. It made the headlines of all the local newspapers and was reported on all of the Baltimore television networks and radio stations. It was a very scary time and the state prosecutors office pulled out all the stops as McDonough promised they would.

They called many of our club members, school teachers and farmers alike, asking them if they had also retained attorneys to represent themselves, implying they were going to be charged as well. They were told to convince us to plead guilty and the charges would be dropped and no further action would be brought against anyone. I knew if they somehow won this case, they would also come after me. They had already let me know I was the target they really wanted. Yet I also knew we had followed the law to the letter and this was only a political prosecution.

We had three really decent and honest circuit court judges in our county and I believed there was no way any of these judges could find us guilty. However, shortly before the trial, we received a disturbing call from our attorney. All three circuit court judges had recused themselves as being too familiar with Sue and me. An out-of-the-county Democrat judge I didn't know anything about was assigned to hear the case.

The state had made a crucial mistake by subpoenaing a representative of the newspaper that had published our ads. They hadn't expected that her testimony would be that the newspaper's legal department had vetted all of our accusations before they agreed to go to print and found the statements we alleged were 100 percent correct. Thankfully, we also had an honest, non-political judge assigned to hear the case. The court found not only were we not guilty, but in fact, were totally innocent of any of the charges brought against us. We were fully exonerated of any wrongdoing whatsoever. On the way out of the courthouse Sue looked at me with a very somber face and asked, "Have we done enough now, can we just go back to work?"

As far as I was concerned, we were done; no more politics. Our business was doing great and I planned to spend most of our time at our Florida residence. That's when something unexpected and even more significant happened that would not only change my life, but the life of every person in the United States. My daughter told me an employee of hers had purchased a house for $750,000 and obtained an almost 100 percent mortgage. She didn't understand how that was possible as her employee's total family income was less than $80,000. Naturally, I assumed that was impossible but just to be sure, I called a friend of mine who knew an official with IndyMac Bank where my daughter's employee acquired her mortgage. My friend called back to say told me it was a "Stated Assets, Stated Income" mortgage. He explained, the Bush administration had twice unsuccessfully opposed the policy, but it was supported by Congressman and Chairman of the House Financial Services Committee, Barney Frank and Senator and Chairman of the Senate Banking Committee, Chris Dodd. They believed anyone who wanted to own a home should be entitled. An overwhelmingly large number of these types of mortgages were being issued by both Fannie Mae and Freddie Mac.

My immediate reaction was this would cause a financial collapse unlike anything this country had ever seen. I asked myself, with it being so incredibly obvious, why in the world would our government have supported it?

I certainly did not want to suffer the same agony I went through in the early 90s, after the commercial real estate downturn, when I owed the banks millions of dollars borrowed against mortgages that had falling real estate values. I knew I had to liquidate as much as I could and as quickly as possible. Working night and day for the next several months I was successful in disposing of enough assets to completely pay off all of my bank loans shortly before the now infamous "Great Recession".

I still had a very healthy net worth, although the lion's share of it was tied up in real estate with their values falling daily. At least I didn't owe a dime to anyone. It is never pleasant losing money, but it was far more unpleasant watching as the liberal lapdog media unfairly blamed President Bush for all of the problems with the economy.

Having been in commercial lending for more than 25 years I had firsthand knowledge of exactly what happened. When President Bush took office in 2001 he ended the recession in its early stage the same way Presidents Coolidge, Kennedy and Reagan had done. He lowered taxes greatly strengthening the economy and generating higher tax revenues. In those few years I witnessed new growth in small business income unlike anything I had ever seen before. Even with the terrible events of 9/11, the economy of the country was strong enough to survive and even continued to thrive.

What happened in late 2006 that would cause the downturn in the economy? Could it possibly have been because both houses of Congress had been won by liberals who believed in a strong entitlement society? Could it have been the fault of those same liberals who believed that every American who wanted to own a home should be entitled to buy it, whether they could afford it or not? Could it have had anything to do with the top executives of Fannie Mae and Freddie Mac collapsing the entire country's real estate market with that insane policy of issuing and guaranteeing loans to millions of people who couldn't afford to make their payments?

Chief Executive Officers James Johnson of Fannie Mae and Franklin Raines of Freddie Mac were extremely well educated and really smart men; why would they possibly do this? Could it have possibly been because these two dedicated loyal CEOs left their offices after making themselves over a mere $110 million? If we had paid them the money and let them stay home it would have been a bargain. Could it have also been the same liberal politicians that supported them were also actually supporting raising fuel and energy costs for every American causing everyone's standard of living to be greatly diminished? No, probably not, it was so much simpler for the so-called main stream media just to blame President George W. Bush.

Chapter 22
Who Is On The Side Of The Angels?

THE 2008 PRESIDENTIAL election was fast arriving. Again, I resisted pressure from many of the political associates and friends I had made over the years to become engaged in either the Republican Primary or the Presidential Election. The extent of my involvement was to attend a few of the McCain-Palin rallies and take some campaign pictures, nothing more. Sue was concerned about my health and I had faithfully promised her that our political activities were all behind us. Besides, I didn't know anyone who knew anything about this new young Senator Barack Obama who had surprised almost everyone when he actually won the Democrat Primary. All of the active Republicans I knew were in fact pleased with his success as they believed Hillary Clinton would have been a much more formidable opponent. Obama also had so much baggage because of his previous questionable associations that many felt McCain would easily win the general election. Personally however, I thought that the contrary was true.

What was not to like about this new young articulate speaker? So much of what he advocated and promised were positions I myself was very passionate about. Though I was not happy when he said that President Bush was unpatriotic for allowing the national debt to increase as much as it had, but the $10 trillion debt was one of my primary concerns as well. Obama promised to cut it in half and that certainly sounded good to me. He said he would lower medical costs for all Americans and his stimulus plan would drive down unemployment levels so that it would be below five

percent again. He said he would control unnecessary spending and promised that lobbyists would not influence his White House. He also promised
a totally bipartisan presidency and said we would see nothing but the utmost of transparency in his administration. This, he told us, was to be the
cleanest administration ever. Our country had become so divided and
Obama said that he was a "uniter" not a divider and I optimistically wondered if he might be the very person who could bring us together. What
was not to like about this man? In some ways, he reminded me of John
Fitzgerald Kennedy, one of my favorite presidents.

Fervently important to me was Obama's promise of energy independence. I foolishly believed that meant exploration for new proven energy
sources here in the United States. As I mentioned before, in the early 1970s
before his death, my father worked in the Executive Office of the White
House as our country's top fuel and energy expert. He had always been a
proud, staunch, liberal Democrat, but even so as a boy I remember how
upset he would get when some people would argue that in Europe they
were paying over a dollar a gallon for gasoline and here in the United States
our cost was about one third of Europe's. Some politicians actually argued
to eliminate what I think was then called the "oil depletion allowance" and
raise taxes at the fuel pump to bring us more in line with Europe. My father's response was always, America is the greatest country in the world and
our economy is far superior to any other place on Earth. Europe is in dire
straits. Why would we possibly want to be more like them? Shouldn't they
try to be more like us? He said the United States greatness was built on
cheap energy and always insisted if we ever lost that, our freedom and very
security would be seriously jeopardized. I believed candidate Obama understood that and although I didn't vote for him, when he won the Presidential
Election I sincerely believed he could become a great president.

It wasn't long before the administration ordered that the oil rigs in the
Gulf be shut down and many were moved out of our country. It was reported those rigs were drilling oil from a depth underwater that was far too
dangerous. After the oil spill, they said it had to be done to protect our environment. I too was concerned about our environment and never questioned their decision. However, I knew how devastating shutting those rigs
down would be for our economy and couldn't imagine how many millions

of Americans were going to be negatively affected. I would have loved to have known my father's thoughts about this, but of course that wasn't possible and I certainly was no expert.

A short time later, it was also reported that the same administration that had ordered the closing of those rigs had guaranteed a loan for $2 billion of our tax dollars to an oil company in Brazil to engage in deep water offshore drilling in the Atlantic just off the Brazilian coastline. Their rigs extended more than three times the depth of the wells that were closed in the Gulf. Did we not share the same environment? Why would they do this? It didn't make sense until I learned that shortly before the United States had made the guarantee, one of President Barack Obama's largest financial supporters during his presidential campaign had invested hundreds of millions of dollars into the same oil company in Brazil. Almost immediately after the announcement of the U.S. financing agreement the company's stock skyrocketed. I'm certain the whole thing was just another big coincidence.

I don't have to tell you how hollow his other promises rang as well. Regulations negatively affecting all businesses, especially small businesses, were being pumped out of this administration by the thousands and no business seemed to be immune. There were so many of these new regulations it was impossible for me to keep up with them. Almost every day, I was receiving calls from my borrowers telling me that their business could survive the bad economy, but not these new burdensome regulations and this was even before "Obamacare." Many who had never missed a payment for years were now finding it difficult to make even partial payments. In my own commercial lending business, the government imposed regulations that made it impossible for me to continue making business loans to small businesses. Good business loans I normally would have issued without hesitation I was forced to decline. My hands were tied. I am absolutely certain that many, if not all of these businesses, would have survived, instead several were forced to close. Many of these business owners had been relying on me for their financing for more than 30 years and now, due to these new regulations, I was unable to help them. Some of them told me that they had actually supported Barack Obama and it hurt me deeply to see the very government they voted for do this to them. I couldn't understand why. A few suggested that the regulations imposed had no purpose other than to empower the government with control over them, which at that time I refused to believe.

Now that I didn't have any debt whatsoever and was not issuing any new loans, I needed to find somewhere to invest the money I was receiving from loans that were being paid off, as many businesses were closing and selling their real estate. I sought advice from my good friend Peter. He explained to me that he was putting much of his money into corporate bonds. He told me that a corporate bond was very similar to the business loans we were doing except instead of being secured by real estate, they were secured by the corporation. He said that if the corporation did go bankrupt, the bondholders were the first to be paid, even before the employees. He suggested I invest in corporate bonds offered by one of the largest companies in the entire world. He believed it was extremely safe because this corporation owned many times the value of the bonds in real estate and other assets. It was inconceivable they would ever go bankrupt, but if they did he said, there was more than enough equity to pay off all of the bondholders in full many times over. What could be safer than that? It was so safe in fact that his broker had invested most of his 401k retirement plan into these bonds.

That was good enough for me. The next couple of payoffs went right into the General Motors bonds he recommended which were later seized by the government and given to Barack Obama's union friends. I viewed it as absolute theft. Thankfully, my loss was small compared to many of my friends who lost millions. Nothing like this had ever happened in the United States before and now I was really concerned.

I couldn't believe that the man who claimed he was going to unite us was now pitting what he considered to be the haves against the have-nots. I viewed it more like the parasites against the hosts. Most people I know are hard-working and not looking for a handout, but this administration wasn't promoting hard work and achievement or even self-reliance. Instead, it was actually encouraging dependency on the government through entitlements. I believe the country had become more polarized now than at any time since the Civil War.

A few years ago, I had taken a tour through the Flagler home mansion which is now a museum in Palm Beach, Florida. The tour guide said that in the 20th century there was no resentment towards the men who achieved personal wealth in America by providing the goods and services that were building our great economic system. She said that people then felt pride in seeing our country become the strongest in the world and that instead of resentment, there was nothing but admiration for Flagler, Edison, Ford, Hearst, Carnegie, Vanderbilt and so many others she named. People saw these men's successes as examples of what they themselves could aspire to achieve only in America. They realized that the possibilities in this country were available to everyone, rich or poor. After all, all of these men started with nothing.

I couldn't help remembering that in 1969 when the real estate financing market had collapsed and I had gone to work selling refrigerators and air conditioners at Sears Roebuck and Company, I had won a weekend trip to California. While there I drove through Beverly Hills. I looked at the beautiful mansions and fancy expensive cars that were everywhere. I didn't feel even a morsel of jealousy or resentment. It only motivated me to get home and learn what successful people were doing in order to emulate them. I thought of the essay written by Ralph Waldo Emerson on self-reliance. "… There is a time in every man's education when he arrives at the conviction that envy is ignorance; that imitation is suicide; that he must take himself for better, for worse, as his portion; that though the wide universe is full of good, no kernel of nourishing corn can come to him but through his toil bestowed on that plot of ground which is given to him to till …"

Never once did I ever expect that the government had a responsibility to provide for me. Our system had provided for its populace the highest standard of living in the world and endless opportunities. In my wildest dreams I couldn't imagine why this administration was changing the course of something that had worked so well in our country for over two centuries.

I could tell you hundreds of other outrageous stories about what's going on in our government, but I'll leave that to the radio and television hosts that have the courage to inform you, and there are some really wonderful ones out there doing it everyday. I had no intention of bringing this administration into my story, but I just couldn't help myself, for it has become such a big part of what surely must now be the twilight years of my life.

I love this country more than anyone can imagine. The freedoms that I was afforded during my lifetime have allowed me to accomplish achievements that could have only been possible here in America. I couldn't feel more indebted to the country that has given me so much and I am grateful for the sacrifices of so many Americans in the last 200 plus years to protect our freedom and spread it throughout the world.

The one thing I've learned best is that most people in our country are basically good. It may surprise you when I say that in spite of all the difficulties we are now facing as a country, I am very optimistic about our future. People in the United States are becoming more connected with our political system than at any other period in my lifetime and that is so important. When I became active in the mid-90s in local county politics, a member of our school board was asked what he thought of Ed Primoff.

He answered, "He's okay, but he's too much into that freedom thing."

It brings me great comfort to now see millions of Americans concerned about that silly old freedom thing. We have and are electing some of the finest leaders we have seen in a long, long time. If you have listened to Dr. Benjamin Carson, you easily recognize the caliber and courage of people that are becoming intricately involved in the political arena. I hope you too feel the same optimism as me.

I was further encouraged when in the summer of 2010, one of my closest friends called to ask if Sue and I would agree to volunteer, as he and his wife had, to clean up the trash that would be left behind after the Restoring Honor rally. To be held at the Lincoln Memorial in August. Even though we had decided that our political involvement was behind us, Sue very much wanted to help and we both wanted to see for ourselves what kind of people would attend the rally. The mainstream media was portraying them as an all-white-gun-toting, Bible-thumping, bunch of freaks and bigots. We were advised that there would probably be no parking available. We drove our car about half-way and finished the trip on the metro. We had attended several events in Washington before but we had never seen the trains so crowded. We had to wait for over an hour to board and when it was finally our turn we were packed in like sardines.

When we arrived I was surprised to see people had come from all parts of the country, as far away as California. They were nothing like the press had portrayed. They were peaceful and polite. Most came as families and their children were incredibly well-behaved. Some people wore patriotic attire while others actually printed on their clothing words displaying their pride in, or love of America. A few carried signs, each hand-made and unique.

I took hundreds of pictures and interviewed several people with my camcorder. I asked my friend, Mike, to see if he could find someone with a sign that exhibited bigotry or was disrespectful in any way. I wanted to photograph and archive all views including the ones the main stream press was so gallantly touting; but neither of us could find or hear anything like what was being reported. Also, unlike what was reported, a good percentage of the crowd was African-Americans, who were very gracious as well.

It was an extremely hot and humid day with people standing shoulder to shoulder for hours. Nevertheless, everyone was really enjoying themselves and delighted to be there. The sunny day was filled with remarkable patriotic speeches and music. It was one of the most inspirational events I had ever attended. We were all quite moved.

After the rally, the four of us, along with the other volunteers, walked with our plastic trash bags through all the fields that hosted the hundreds of thousands of attendees. The lawns looked manicured and not one of us could find even a single piece of trash left behind. On our return aboard the metro we were all pretty tired and the crowded car was now very quiet. I looked over at my friends, Mike and Diane. Diane held her hand over her face in an attempt to conceal her emotion; but I could see she had tears in her eyes.

I asked her, "What is wrong?"

"I've never been so proud to be an American."

About a month after the Restoring Honor rally, Mike called me again and suggested we go to another rally in October. It was called "One Nation Working Together." Sponsors included the A.F.L.-C.I.O., Service Employees International Union (SEIU), National Council of La Raza, Sierra Club and others. It also was to be held at the Lincoln Memorial. The *New York Times* reported that there was, "A sea of yellow, red, blue and purple T-shirts stretching out below, worn by members of various civil rights, peace and union groups."

That was very true almost everyone wore colorful T-shirts with their union names printed on them. It appeared that the large majority of people there were bused in. A union member told us that the T-shirts and buses were provided by her union. As people arrived, many were handed professionally printed signs to carry throughout the rally. Frankly, we were shocked to see people proudly displaying many of these signs; some of which I would refer to as, anti-American messages. Many read, "Capitalism is failing, Socialism is the alternative." Others read, "Remember the FBI targeted Dr. King, stop FBI attacks against antiwar and union activist;" "U.S. and Israel nuclear weapons out of the middle east! Hands off Iran;" "Medicare for all;" "It's your fight too;" "Working together for immigrant rights;" "A new urgency in the struggle for world socialism;" and many, many others. All of these were professionally printed. Also professionally printed political type buttons were offered for them to wear that read, "MARX was Right," and "For Profit Healthcare Makes Me Sick."

I can't say that everyone there supported these views. In fact some of the people I spoke with specifically said they did not and were offended by the signs, but it appeared to us that the overwhelming majority of them did agree.

Many people brought provisions for their lunch and when the rally was over there was partially eaten food, paper bags, cups and garbage everywhere. Even the water in the fountain at the World War II Memorial was littered with paper debris from fast food and waste. In front of the overwhelming amount of trash on the lawn of the Washington Monument, there was a sign posted by the National Park Service which read, "Trash Free Zone, Please Respect Your National Park."

The main theme of the rally seemed to be to get out the vote so the Democrats could maintain control over both houses in the 2010 election which was only a month away. Their efforts were in vain. As you know, they were not successful.

Not only did the conservatives take back control of the U.S. House of Representatives, but in my local Carroll County election there were major changes as well. Because of concerns over out-of-control corruption with the sitting commissioners, two local businessmen engaged in a massive effort to institute a totally new form of government in the county. Both of them were good friends of mine and each told me that they had been advised by their attorneys and almost everyone they knew that it would be almost impossible to achieve and they were only wasting their time. They refused to submit to defeat and motivated with determination they actually were successful in achieving it through a referendum. Instead of three commissioners being elected at-large, the county was divided into five districts. Now each commissioner had to stand on their own and run for office in their home district where they were best known. Gouge had three opponents. One was a teenager and I personally never thought he took his candidacy seriously. Gouge received the least votes of anyone in her district, including the teenager. The county now had five new commissioners and I could not have been more pleased.

There were signs that an incredibly large number of Americans throughout the country were not going to sit idle any longer. Almost everyone knows that contempt for the Christian religion had been common in many places throughout the world for a long time, but no one believed they would see it here in the United States of America.

I was surprised by the unleashed outrage from the left when Dan Cathy, President of Chick-fil-A simply stated to the Baptist Press of the Southern Baptist Convention that he supported the biblical definition of the family unit. He was merely responding to a question about his definition of marriage, yet he was painted as an anti-gay bigot. There seems to be no end to their vile, unfounded personal attacks.

Cathy further fueled the left's outrage when he stated that, "his company was a family-owned and led business giving thanks to God that they were married to their first wives."

Radical leftists throughout the country were going as far as to call for boycotts of his business. When Cathy was advised that his statements could negatively affect his business and asked if he actually said and believed his words, he did not back down and replied, "Guilty as charged."

The *Chicago Sun-Times* reported that Mayor and former White House Chief of Staff for Obama, Rahm Emanuel said, "Chick-fil-A's values are not Chicago values" and hinted strongly that he was prepared to join in blocking them from opening its first freestanding Chicago store in Logan Square. I believe this incident, as well as the other radical ideologies of the left, may have led to a turning point. Millions of Americans, who for the most part had been silent up until then, had now had enough of the leftist radicals trying to force their morality, or should I say immorality, on the rest of us. In many locations throughout the country people waited in line for hours at their local Chick-fil-A to show support for Cathy. Personally, I had never eaten at one before, but in West Palm Beach, Sue and I waited almost two hours in line. Actually my lunch was really good, and they have caffeine free diet soda which is usually not served in restaurants. Now I eat there often and I am certain Chick-fil-A has many other new loyal customers.

The leftist movement backfired. I believe the type of changes that they are trying to impose on America will also backfire. People who had never been politically engaged in the past are now becoming concerned with the direction of our country and paying more attention than they had before. Look at what happened in September 2013. Who would've believed that in liberal New York City popular Anthony Weiner and Eliot Spitzer, both initially in first place in the polls, would be so soundly defeated in the Democratic Primary for Mayor and Comptroller, respectively. That same day, Colorado's Senate President John Morse and State Senator Angela Giron were ousted from office, in spite of the $350,000 contribution made by New York City Mayor Michael Bloomberg to a Colorado committee formed to defeat the recall vote of each. Both senators were replaced by conservative Republicans.

The spokeswoman for the recall, Jennifer Kerns, said "It's about government overreach, and sends a reverberating message across the country that people are sick of it."

America has had many downturns in the past but always came back stronger than ever and I have little doubt that this time we will as well. As one of my closest friends Don Messenger said just recently before passing away, "We are on the side of the angels."

Chapter 23
Being Nobody But Yourself

WELL, MY STORY is coming to its completion and as I told you in the beginning, I didn't really know how to write it, therefore, I don't know how to end it without just dying. I'd rather not do that for the time being. There can't possibly be much sand left in my hourglass anyway. Being so blessed, I don't want to leave without passing on to you the most important lessons I have been fortunate to learn in my lifetime.

Before I started my story, I told you that anyone in America can achieve anything they really want and that hasn't changed. You don't have to be very smart to succeed; I'm living proof of that. I have discovered that all successful people seem to share the same exact characteristics. I want to tell you what differentiates them from the others, but first let me give you my favorite definition of success that I heard on an old phonograph recorded by Earl Nightingale almost 50 years ago: "Success is the progressive realization of a worthy ideal."

It doesn't necessarily have anything to do with making money. In my lifetime, I believe one of the most successful women in the world was Mother Teresa. Is there anyone who would disagree? If the success you seek is financial, academic, physical, or whatever, it doesn't matter. The prerequisites to succeed are always the same.

Don't think for a minute that because of all the new burdensome regulations imposed by the current administration that there are now no opportunities available to you. Sure, I'll be the first to tell you it's harder now than ever before. Many small business owners have felt compelled to close and many have closed their businesses. Conditions now are very similar to those in 1980 when companies were closing by the thousands and yet I made more money that year than at any other time in my life.

There are now, and will always be, many new opportunities. I recently learned that there were more millionaires made during the Great Depression then before. Using this poor economy not to fulfill your dreams is only an excuse. Let me give you a couple of examples of people who recently refused to accept failure.

For several years, I had the pleasure of financing transactions for one of the nicest and most honest young businessman I had ever dealt with. Scott was in the home improvement business in Maryland and was also beginning to purchase many homes and remodeling them for resale. He was doing quite well until about three years ago when the real estate market collapsed and he was left with a few properties that were worth considerably less than he had paid for them. He could have easily given up and simply blamed the economy for his misfortune, but he didn't do that. Instead, after going through a short period of depression, he sought and found opportunities in an entirely new business.

I was very fond of this young man and was so proud when he called to tell me how wonderful he was doing in the first year of his new venture. By the end of the second year he had more than 30 employees in this new business and his personal income was now higher than it was in the best of times in his previous business. I spoke with him this past December and he was finishing up his third year. He was excited to tell me that even in this bad economy, his business had grown to such an extent that his income was now into the seven figures, something he had never accomplished before.

Another business acquaintance, who became a very good friend, lives in San Diego, California. He too had become so displeased with the state of the economy and what it had done to his business that he actually purchased a home in Costa Rica and planned to move there. Realizing it was going to take at least a year to sell his home and complete the transfer, he started a new temporary business right there in San Diego. He told me that his new business had done extremely well last year and is now doing even better. He said he canceled his plans to move and will use the Costa Rica home as a vacation getaway.

These are just some examples of several people I know who are doing quite well. I know what characteristics these people possess that enables them to succeed while others do not, even in this terrible economy. In the past 30 years when I interviewed owners of small businesses I could predict almost with 100 percent certainty who would succeed and who would not. Before completing my story, I feel compelled to share with you what the most important characteristics are that every successful person I have known had in common. It doesn't matter if we are talking about making money, being the best fit person in the gym, or being at the top of your academic class. The same principles always apply and you won't read about them in most self-help books.

It has become obvious to me that the most important prerequisite in achieving whatever it is you want is that you must be willing to do what most other people are not willing to do. You cannot imagine how many times people have told me how much smarter they believed they were than someone else in their same business, yet they were making much less money. Often I would agree that they were smarter, but I would always ask them, "What is it that they are doing that you are not?"

They would seldom have an answer. Then I would tell them exactly what the other person was doing. I usually would get a response something like, "I'm not willing to do that; no way."

Almost as important is the level of your desire to succeed. I never met anyone who wanted to fail. Everyone has a desire to succeed at whatever they're doing, but that's not nearly enough. Your desire to succeed at whatever you want to accomplish must be the strongest and most important emotion in your life. Don't misunderstand me, I'm not telling you this is the right thing for you. I'm only letting you know what is necessary to guarantee your success and that this is a characteristic shared by every single successful person I know. What is important to you is only for you to decide.

Over the years many of my friends told me that they thought I placed far too much importance on my business and not enough on pleasure. When I graduated from high school my grandmother gave me a card that contained a check. Far more important than the check were the words she wrote quoting Henry Wadsworth Longfellow. The money was soon gone, but the words have always stayed with me. "The heights of great men reached and kept were not attained by sudden flight, but they, while their companions slept, were toiling upward in the night."

The United States Department of Health and Human Services reported that in this, the greatest country in the world, "95 percent of the people in this country do not achieve financial independence by age of 65, but rather they end up dependent on the government, or charity, or their families, or they have to keep working until they die." I never wanted to be there. Many of the same friends that criticized me are now struggling in their senior years. Sure, I worked hard and made a lot of sacrifices, but in the final analysis the financial independence for me and my family brings me an immense amount of gratification.

Another thing I've learned about people that are succeeding at whatever they are doing is that they don't have excuses. I'm sure you've heard someone say, "He has that magic touch," or "Everything he touches turns to gold." Think of someone you know like that. Has anyone ever told you that they were going to do something and later gave you an excuse after they did not accomplish it?

I find there are basically two kinds of people in the world. Some get things done and others have excuses why they couldn't. Usually they are really good excuses and difficult to argue with. Someone tells you that they're going to meet you at three o'clock. They don't show up, but later tell you that while driving to meet you they got caught in traffic. How can you possibly argue with that? It's a great excuse, but haven't you noticed that some people just get things done while others always have great excuses?

In 2005 I hired a contractor to construct an addition onto my Florida home. The first three times he was to be at my home with his crew he didn't show up, but he always had a great excuse, and I mean it, they really were great excuses. Eventually, I found another contractor who did show up and he never had an excuse. A couple of years later we were at the mall in Wellington, Florida and guess who pulled up right beside us? It was the first contractor and on the side of his truck was a sign that read, "Small Engine Repair." Not surprisingly, he was no longer in the contracting business.

There is something else I'd like to pass on to you. Ever since I was a very small child people told me all the things I couldn't accomplish. I can remember some of my teachers telling me that I had to be more like the other children. My mother was told at a PTA meeting that I was always trying to do things differently than the other children and I needed to learn to conform to do things in the same way all the other children were doing them. Even my father, who I loved very much, told me I could never be successful at selling real estate. The broker in my first real estate job didn't believe I could get business by knocking on doors and I was only wasting my time. Actually, I think there was always someone to discourage and pressure me not to do almost everything I've done in my entire life.

I was not blessed to have grandchildren, but if I did, I would teach them to learn from the words of great thinkers like E.E. Cummings who said, "To be nobody but yourself, in a world which is doing its best, night and day, to make you like everybody else, means to fight the hardest battle which any human being can fight, and never stop fighting."

Now that I have learned about the 95 percent of all people in this country that are not even financially independent at age 65, I realize that most of those people criticizing and discouraging me were among that group. I'm not saying that you can't learn from others; of course you can and should. I have learned something from everyone I've ever known, but I've always done what I believed was right for me, regardless of what others thought or said. Life is very precious, you only get one shot at it.

Every day should be an exciting adventure. Take time to evaluate all of your decisions and always have the courage to do what you believe in your heart is right for you. I was always impressed and have never forgotten the quote of poet John Greenleaf Whittier, "Of all the sad words of tongue or pen, the saddest are these, 'It might have been'."

The great singer and songwriter Jackson Brown put it this way:

> Just do the steps that you've been shown
> By everyone you've ever known
> Until the dance becomes your very own
> No matter how close to yours
> Another's steps have grown
> In the end there is one dance you'll do alone

The bottom line is that we live in a great country, the greatest in the world. Here the sky's the limit, if you can think it, you can do it. I have little doubt in my mind that if I had to start all over again I would have no difficulty surpassing where I am today. Of course I'd need a little time and I probably don't have that, but hopefully you do.

Chapter 24
What Is Really Most Important?

BEFORE MY STORY comes to an end there is still one thing I have to tell you. Until recently no one other than Sue knew that I was writing my life's experiences. Later, I did tell a couple of my very closest friends. Some warned me not to include this last chapter and were emphatic that if I did, it would have zero chance of ever being published. That may very well be true, but without including it, everything else is meaningless.

As a very young child, when my bedroom was completely engulfed in flames, I suffered only minor burns. When I fell more than 30 feet and broke both my legs, the doctors said it was a miracle I survived at all, let alone acquired no permanent injuries. When I was in the Air Force my first wife and I were taking a quiet afternoon ride through Folsom State Park in California. The road had many turns and the speed limit was 20 miles per hour. The accident report stated that the skid marks had revealed that I was driving at a speed of 15 miles per hour and was in my lane traveling around a turn. The oncoming car, which had crossed into my lane, was traveling at more than 50 miles per hour. I think I was unconscious for only a few seconds, but when I regained consciousness the other driver was lying on the ground bleeding profusely from multiple wounds. I saw my ex-wife tearing much of her clothing into strips and tying them around his wounds to stop the bleeding, probably saving his life. I ran more than two miles back to the check-in station to summon emergency services. As they took the other driver away in an ambulance the responders said that they couldn't believe my ex-wife or I received even as much as a scratch.

About a year later, while still in the Air Force, a good friend and fellow airman, Joe Ortega, and I pulled an all-nighter. Both of us being stupid teenagers, were driving back to the base on Highway Route 50 at about 5:00 a.m. I was awakened with Joe frantically screaming as he reached over and turned the steering wheel away from the telephone pole that was directly in front of us, only seconds before impact at about 65 miles an hour. The entire right side of my beautiful 1952 Pontiac was demolished and the car was totaled. Joe and I however received no injuries whatsoever.

Years later back in Maryland, married with a child, I clearly had an abundant residual of teenage immaturity. When the chemicals blew up in my face, the doctors couldn't understand why the glass Pyrex pitcher didn't explode into thousands of small particles which would have caused disastrous damage and could have even killed me.

When the control cable broke in the twin-engine airplane as we were landing at Baltimore-Washington International Airport, the FAA reported that this type of incident almost always ended with fatalities. Was it just a coincidence that we were saved by a simple little gopher hole just before crashing into the high tension airport equipment?

A few years after that experience Sue and I were flying a single engine Beechcraft Bonanza back to Maryland after taking my eight-year-old daughter and her girlfriend on a three-day vacation to Florida. The four of us took off from Fort Lauderdale in what is called, IFR conditions, "Instrument Flight Rules." The clouds were very thick, but I felt comfortable as the weather service reported that the ceilings were at 8,000 feet and we would be flying somewhat higher than that in a clear blue sky. We expected a beautiful smooth ride home. Unfortunately, as we approached 10,000 feet we were still in the clouds and weather conditions had become much worse than the forecasters had expected. About 30 minutes into the flight and just outside Orlando our engine completely shut down. Frantic, as I attempted unsuccessfully to restart the engine, I alerted the control center and requested an emergency landing at Orlando airport. The response I received was quite frightening.

"Orlando airport is closed, conditions are zero, zero."

We could see nothing through our windows except dark gray and I knew this could end very badly. In this situation you don't see anything until you hit it. I turned to a heading of due east hoping for the possibility of at least making the shoreline. At our descent rate it took several minutes to reach 800 feet which seemed more like hours, before the engine began to spit, sputter and finally started. We landed safely at the first available airport.

When the bank in Virginia sued me for nonpayment of someone else's loan, we acquired the documents needed to prove that their charges were totally false just a few days before the trial only because the bank had mistakenly given us their confidential file. What were the chances of that happening?

These are only a few examples of the many troubles I've experienced throughout my life, but remarkably none of them had an unpleasant conclusion and somehow, contrary to all the medical experts, I still can put a little fog on the mirror every morning.

My favorite of all the mathematic courses I have taken and the one I did best in was, "Permutations, Calculations, and Probability." There is no way of mathematically calculating the probability that the tribulations in my life would have concluded as they did with remarkably positive results simply by coincidence; but one doesn't have to know mathematics at all to know it would be impossible to have transpired by happenstance.

About a year ago one of my oldest and closest friends, Tom a retired professor, called and asked me what I was trying to pull. At first I thought he was kidding and I asked what he was talking about. Earlier we had dinner with him, his wife and several other friends when someone asked if any of us believed there was really a God. At the time I had no idea it bothered Tom so much when I answered, "I have absolutely no doubt, He's been with me all of my life."

Tom was calling wanting to know why I answered like that. He really was very angry and said that I was the smartest person he knew and surely must know science had proven God was only a myth. I told him I was very disappointed that he was of that opinion and I believed that the reason our country is now having so many problems is because you professors are teaching that nonsense to our children. I told him I recently heard a lecture from one of our country's most respected scientists who said that he had been an atheist all his life, as were his parents. When he became famous for his study of DNA, he said he was going to use it to prove there was no God. Instead, he said he proved there was a God.

I told Tom that I could not explain it as well as he did, but let me put it this way:

You know what every substance in your car is, steel, fabric, etc. What are the possibilities that a volcano would erupt and the molten lava flowing down the mountain would melt some rubber trees forming tires? Berries would be turned into paint and ore would become steel. Some of the molten rubber would harden around copper and become wire. All of this would come together at the bottom of the mountain and there would be a beautiful automobile with key in it ready to go? I asked Tom what he thought the possibility of that was.

He said that was the most ridiculous thing he had ever heard.

I said no Tom; scientists tell us that the human body is more than a million times more complicated than your car. Our bodies contain more than 200,000 tiny computers all dependent on each other. The fact that you think this all happened by accident is the most ridiculous thing I've ever heard, and I can't believe you really think otherwise. Tom knows I am Jewish, but I told him that this great country we live in was founded on the teachings of Jesus Christ and regardless of anyone's beliefs, only a fool could believe that there is not a divine creator.

I asked Tom if he had ever gone out of his way to really help someone and then they showed no gratitude at all. How did that make him feel? He said it has not happened often, but when it does it really makes him angry.

I asked him, suppose for a moment there is a Creator, whoever he or she may be, and consider all the things he's done for you. You have had a great life, how do you think he feels about your ungratefulness?

He responded by saying he would bet his life that there was no Creator. I told him that was exactly what he was doing.

I realized that there was no reasoning with Tom. I had known and loved Tom and his wife for more than 40 years. It hurt and scared me that he had been so poisoned by our current educational system.

When he began quoting Bill Ayers, the radical professor who founded the Weather Underground movement and bombed the Pentagon in the 1960s and is now an unrepentant tenured professor, our conversation was over. We haven't spoken with each other since. I can understand that there are people foolish enough to believe that there is no creator. What I can't understand is why they are so strongly compelled to convince everyone else of their belief.

Maybe my friends were right when they said this part of my life should not be included in my story, but how could I possibly not include the things that are most important to me? We have been blessed to live in the greatest country in the world. Just over 200 years ago, the architects of our constitution, who by the way were almost all fervent believers, provided for us the best system of government in the world.

All of my life, even at times after I had attained financial security, I continued to work aggressively. I did so not because I wanted bigger and better things, but because I worried there would come a time when I would not be able to support myself or my family. I tell you this so that you will understand how unfounded my concerns were. I feel kind of like what Mark Twain said, "I'm an old man and have known a great many troubles, but most of them never happened."

What I've come to realize, almost better than anything else, is that anyone willing to work and follow a few basic principles can obtain any level of success they desire. I can't stress enough that in this country, the only handicap you have is the one in your mind. However, what I've also observed throughout my life is that the people who are grateful for what they have, and to their Creator, whoever that might be to them, live a much happier and more fulfilled life.

Image Gallery

Ed Primoff

Living in the apartment above this laundry was not pleasant but it
saved me a lot of money.

My sisters Wanda and JoAnne with me in the early 1950s.

Teenage Years

Civil Air Patrol

First Achievement

High School Picture

My Father

Dad's Card

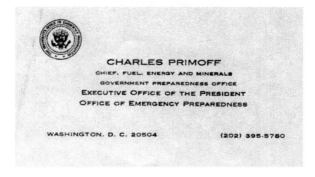

CHARLES PRIMOFF
CHIEF, FUEL, ENERGY AND MINERALS
GOVERNMENT PREPAREDNESS OFFICE
EXECUTIVE OFFICE OF THE PRESIDENT
OFFICE OF EMERGENCY PREPAREDNESS

WASHINGTON, D. C. 20504   (202) 395-5780

Dad's Obituary

C 6   *Monday, Dec. 11, 1972*   THE WASHINGTON POST

CHARLES PRIMOFF

**U.S. Board
Specialist
On Energy**

Charles Primoff, 56, an official with the Office of Emergency Preparedness, died yesterday at George Washington University Hospital after undiagnosed surgery.

He was chief adviser on oil

Me and My Mother

The award for my idea for modifications of all transport vehicles presented with wrinkles and creases.

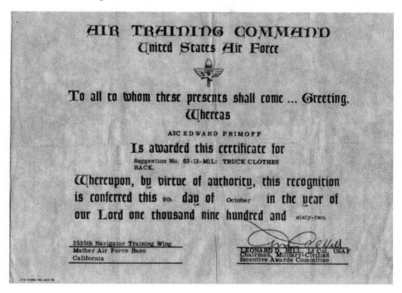

The book that started me on my way.

Laundry Route Contest 1964

Contest News

August 20, 1964

As we begin to go into the last few weeks of our contests, we find that each new customer is beginning to "count big" towards deciding our winners.

The outstanding effort of the past week was by Ed Primoff (#8). Ed scored a total of 298 points. This enabled him to take over 1st place in both his group and the entire contest. Ed has a total of 1019 points...280 more than his nearest competitor. Jack Bigby #72.

Group Standings

Daniels (2)-488	Bigby(72)----739	Cleaveland(38)-275
Toth (10)---457	Buchanan(18)-512	Davis(36)------256
King (34)---347	Brady(33)--- 389	Mehalic(61)----239

Burns(57)-----500	Hewitt(74)-567	Shreve(16)-----529
Riggs(12)-----313	Melvin(15)-220	Miller(44)-----332
Pastelnick(4)-228	Taylor(41)-210	Dawson(52)-----287

Primoff(8)--1019	Dawson(76)-----351
Holmes(74)-- 701	Galleher(24)---211
Garner(51)-- 501	Hungerford(50)-204

Reminder: 1st place...$100.00; 2nd place...$50.00; 3rd..$25.00
Plus vacation to top man of all groups....

****

Increase Contest

Charles Holmes (75) still leads the Increase Contest. Holmes has exceeded his quota by plus 23.0%. Ed Primoff (8) is close behind Holmes with plus 19.8%.

The only prize for the increase contest is $50.00 cash to the leader of each group. The leaders are:

Daniels (2)...-5.7		Roberson (58)..... 5.3
Bigby (72)....11.3		Miller(44),...... 8.0
Davis (36)....- .40		Holmes (75),...... 23.0
Burns(57).....-3.3		J. Dawson(76),,...- 5.6

Plus vacation to the man showing largest increase...

****

SALES MEETING

THERE WILL BE A GENERAL SALES MEETING ON WEDNESDAY, AUGUST 26TH AT 2:30 PM. ALL SALESMEN ARE TO ATTEND..

(SEE NEXT PAGE)

A few of my Wear-Ever sales awards.

Pay Check Stubs 1965

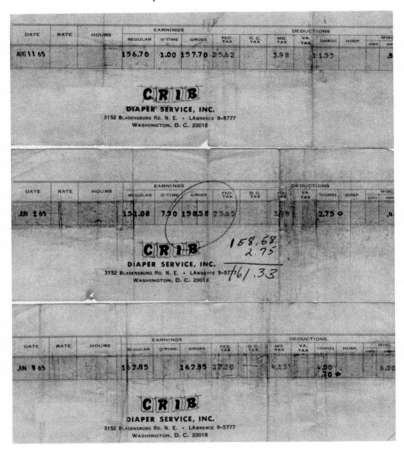

My Darling Daughter Krissy

Recent Photo of Krissy and Me

Me before experimental intestinal bypass surgery...

...and then only eight months later.

First Airplane

Some of the other airplanes we have owned.

Sue flies our Bonanza while taking pictures of me flying our new turbo 310.

The old 310 at the scene of the accident at Baltimore
Washington International Airport.

Not Quite The Gentleman Farmer

Robert Slack, me and Dr. John Slack with the money clip returned to
President Reagan.

"Annie" proves to me you're never without love if you have a dog.

Me introducing gubernatorial candidate, U. S. Congressman Robert Ehrlich.

RG EAGLE

Volume 1, Number 19

Large Crowd Welcomes Ehrlich

"When I'm governor, the vindictiveness towards Carroll County will end."
- Republican Gubernatorial Candidate, U.S. Congressman Robert Ehrlich

Republican Commissioner candidate Ed Primoff (holding microphone) introduces gubernatorial candidate and U.S. Congressman Robert Uhrlich, at a political fundraiser last Saturday, August 24. At left is Congressman Roscoe Bartlett and at right is Lt. Governor candidate Michael Steele. The stage was set up inside Primoff's airplane hanger at his Woodbine home.

An estimated crowd of over 800 came to Ed and Sue Primoff's Woodbine estate to give an enthusiastic show of support for Republican gubernatorial candidate Robert warmly received, as was his running mate Michael Steele. In his brief remarks, Ehrlich promised a new day of cooperation for Carroll County when he is elected

Robert Ehrlich announcing Michael Steele (left) as his running mate.

Ehrlich wins Maryland Governorship.

Robert Ehrlich walks out to be inaugurated Governor of Maryland.

Restoring Honor rally 2010
(Note pristine grounds and WWII Memorial)

Union Sponsored "One NationWorking Together" rally, 2010.
(Note garbage strewn through out the grounds.)

Rally in Palm Beach Florida 2000, supporting Bush in the
days of the "hanging chad".

DC rally during the re-count of the 2000 election.

Barbara Olson

First Lady Laura Bush tears up as the President speaks about 9/11.

2004 Republican Convention Madison Square Garden
President George W. Bush, First Lady Laura Bush, Vice
President Dick Cheney and his wife Liz Cheney

Condoleezza Rice at the Republican National Convention 2004

President Bush and First Lady Laura Bush. Florida election 2004 with
Governor Jeb Bush, First Daughters Barbara and Jenna Bush working at
campaign headquarters in Palm Beach County, Florida.
Lower right: Sue greets Vice President Dick Cheney

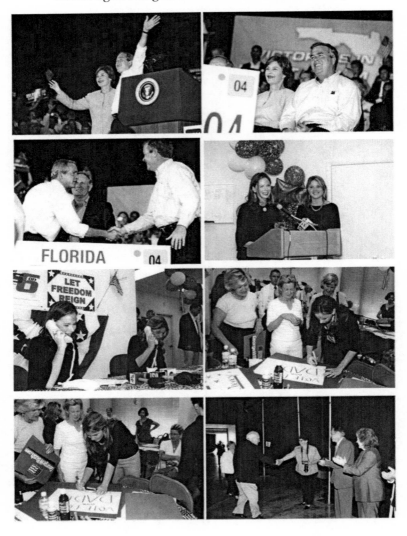

From top left to right: Interior Secretary Gale Norton and me, me with
Karl Rove, Doro Bush Koch and me, Oliver North with us, artist Thomas
Kinkade and Sue, Michael Steele and Doro Bush Koch, me with
Condoleezza Rice, Jack Kemp and me.

It was fun being at the home of James Carville and Mary Matalin.

Top: Deputy Social Secretary Jeanie Figg, left with U.S. Marine Corps Band

Bottom: Max Doeblér, center, oversees the entire all volunteer White House Military Aides

It was always a thrill to get our photo with the first couple. Photo at lower right was taken in the lower Cross Hall of the White House.

Deputy Social Secretary, Jeanie Figg assists Karl Rove with one of his extra duties at the White House.

I loved "First Dog" Barney

Good times photos

The President and Mrs. Bush on the South Lawn.

The President always honored us with a friendly wave.

Sue with Augusta Petrone, Karl Rove and Ambassador Joseph Petrone.

Me with Social Secretary Cathy Fenton, center, Deputy Social
Secretary Jeanie Figg (to the right) and staff.

Sue and Laura Bush share a laugh.

Famous White House Chef Roland Mesnier presents Sue
with a birthday cake featuring our three dogs.

Sue in the White House East Wing Social Office and convention.

House Speaker Nancy Pelosi enjoyed the White House events.

Conga line at the Congressional Ball.

The beauty of the White House at Christmas

Sue and I before and after Christmas events at the White House.

Row 1: Garth Brooks; Meryl Streep. Row 2: Naomi Judd, Dick Cheney; Jack Nicholson. Row 3: Me with a beauty; Left to right, Frank Perdue, Dr. Romona Ortega, Jane Russell, Mitzi Perdue.

It was truly an honor to be photographed with Bill O'Reilly.

Me pretending to be important.

White House residence staff enjoys clowning with the
President before the official photograph.

Steve Doocy goofing with Shepard Smith, both of Fox News.

Steve Doocy joked on his Fox & Friends show the next morning
that Sue was so nice he gave her "the dip" to take home.

Molly Hanneberg and Brian Kilmeade of Fox News.

The great Rush Limbaugh.

Sue Greets Jim Angle

Two Members of Congress enjoy a dance at the Congressional Ball.

Oprah Winfrey, who looked positively stunning, converses with Robert Redford at the White House reception for the Kennedy Center honorees, December, 2005.

Kennedy Center Honoree Elton John

Defense Secretary and Mrs. Donald Rumsfeld enjoying a
conversation with Kennedy Center honoree Warren Beatty.

Known as "The Most Trusted Man in America," Walter Cronkite.

Row 1: Neil Cavuto with Bill O'Reilly; Sue with Sean Hannity.
Row 2: Shepard Smith, Sue and Bret Baier; Wolf Blitzer. Row 3:
Sue with Bill Plante; Sue with wonderful Willard Scott. Row 4:
Sue with Ann Compton; Me with the one and only Tim Russert.

Out of all the photos I took of President Bush, this is my favorite.

Sue's invitation from First Lady Laura Bush.

THE WHITE HOUSE

Mrs. Sue Primoff

Mrs. Bush
requests the pleasure of your company
at a coffee to be held at
The White House
on Wednesday, January 24, 2001
at ten o'clock

I am truly proud of and grateful for the medals I received
for my photo work from the military and service groups
during my years at the White House.

Mrs. Bush was always so gracious.

These are just two of the many letters she sent us.

Laura Bush

December 18, 2002

Mrs. Edward Primoff
7201 Old Washington Post
Woodbine, Maryland 21797

Dear Sue,

Thank you and Ed very much for the adorable photo of
Barney. President Bush and I are thrilled to have it and
look forward to displaying it in our hallway filled with
family photos.

Thanks, too, for the time you both have contributed to
helping with the White House holiday receptions. We
greatly appreciate your generosity!

The President joins me in sending many thanks and best
wishes for a wonderful holiday season.

Sincerely,

Laura Bush

THE WHITE HOUSE

January 31, 2005

Mr. and Mrs. Edward Primoff
Post Office Box 385
Sykesville, Maryland 21784-0385

Dear Sue and Ed,

The albums of photos from the Republican Convention are
fabulous! I admire your talent as a photographer and am
grateful for your generosity

President Bush and I greatly appreciate your volunteer service at
the holiday parties. You kept the photograph lines moving
smoothly and made the festivities more fun for our guests and
for us.

We send our best wishes for a happy 2005.

With warm regards,

Laura Bush

Our last night view of the East Entrance taken from our
designated parking area.

Our residences (top) in Florida and (bottom) Maryland summer farm ranch with FAA approved runway in foreground.

CPSIA information can be obtained at www.ICGtesting.com
Printed in the USA
BVOW05s2216040814

361682BV00001B/18/P